R.K. NARAYAN
Critical Perspectives

"Narayan has no axes of any kind: he is that rare
thing in India today, a man of letters pure and simple."

—*K. R. Srinivasa Iyengar*

A New Series from STERLING

CRITICAL STUDIES ON LITERARY WRITERS

R.K. NARAYAN
Critical
Perspectives

Edited by
A.L. McLeod

STERLING PUBLISHERS PRIVATE LIMITED

STERLING PUBLISHERS PRIVATE LIMITED
L-10, Green Park Extension, New Delhi-110016

R.K. Narayan: Critical Perspectives
© 1994, A.L. McLeod
ISBN : 81 207 1623 x

PRINTED IN INDIA

Published by S.K. Ghai, Managing Director, Sterling Publishers Pvt. Ltd., New Delhi-110016. Laserset at Queff Computers & Communication (P) Ltd., New Delhi. Printed at Ram Printograph (India), New Delhi-110002.

PREFACE

R.K. Narayan is arguably India's most famous author — and its most accomplished. Some, such as Rabindranath Tagore, Mohandas K. Gandhi, and Jawaharlal Nehru, may have attained greater stature for a brief time or exerted greater influence on world events or national politics, but as a writer *per se*, none has worked with such great acclaim in so many genres for such a long period and with so great renown.

Narayan's writing spans the greatest period of change in modern Indian history, from the declining days of the British raj (*Swami and Friends*, 1935) to the present (*The World of Nagaraj*, 1990), during which he has published over a dozen novels that have established his fictional Malgudi as the Indian equivalent of Thomas Hardy's Wessex, William Faulkner's Yoknapatawpha, or Patrick White's Sarsaparilla. In addition, he has retold the great Indian legends and myths and written in contemporary English the great epics, the *Ramayana* and the *Mahabharata*. Further, he has published five collections of short stories, two collections of reportage and personal essays, three travel books, and a memoir — in addition to many feature articles for newspapers, journals and magazines. That is, for over half a century he has been an indefatigable and versatile writer in English, and he has increasingly attracted an international, sophisticated readership in addition to his loyal following of Indian readers. And as the years have passed, Narayan has received critical attention from the academic community, who see in his work much more than simple narrative fiction, stories to amuse and to help pass time agreeably; they see in him, moreover, a writer who transcends the regional and national and writes (though almost always about India and from an Indian perspective) about mankind and for readers everywhere.

Narayan belongs to the same generation as W.H. Auden, Graham Greene, Evelyn Waugh, Rex Warner and Anthony Powell; like them, he early established himself as a literary stylist — though his style is discernibly different from theirs and from that of the three Indian contemporaries whose work he has frequently praised: Raja Rao, Mulk Raj Anand and Balachandra Rajan. All of these writers, he has pointed out, were brought up on Dickens, Thackeray, Hardy, Austen and Scott— masters of English prose style, though different from each other. And Narayan's achievement clearly is the more remarkable, because English is for him an acquired language: his native languages are Tamil (from the Madras area) and Kannada (from Mysore). Yet he is concerned about the future of English as a literary language in India at present, especially because of the government-promoted preference for Hindi and local languages. In an interview with J. Anthony Lukas in 1965, he said, "Writing, at least in the English language, is not in a very good way here these days. The teaching of English in our schools and universities is simply deplorable. I don't want to say, 'after me the deluge,' but I am afraid that my generation is the last which will produce English writing of an international standard in India." In South India this prediction may seem to have greater probability than elsewhere, for there are decreasing numbers of people for whom English is a first language or who can be said to have native language competency, and the characteristic Indian solecisms are quickly promoting the development of a dialect analogous to West Indian English.

In a monograph in the *Writers and Their Work* series some twenty years ago, William Walsh commented that Narayan's novels are "comedies of sadness," and he concluded that "Narayan's fastidious art, blending exact realism, poetry, melancholy, perception and gaiety, is without precedent in English literature and as far as one can see, without following. It is engaging because of the charm and authenticity of its Indian setting, moving because of the substantial, universal human nature which it incarnates" (23). In the years since, there have been numerous studies of Narayan's work from an ever-widening group of scholars, each sharing enthusiasms and insights, making analyses and comparisons and isolating special strengths or developments. All have helped others and have assisted in the general appreciation of the writer's work. However, in a letter addressed to the participants in conference on his work held at the Institute for Commonwealth and American Studies in Mysore in January 1992, Narayan wrote :

I feel that no one should read too much meaning or significance into my writing. I write because I have no other business in life and I also enjoy the sense of relief after finishing a book, although it may involve continuous obsession with a single theme or character all hours of the day (and sometimes night, too) to the extent of about 70,000 words or less, and at the end I feel like a schoolboy at the end of his examinations.

I must admit at the same time that the sense of relief is tinged with regret at parting company from a character after months and months of association. But I value the whole exercise as an experience; and if you feel, as a reader, the same sense of experience; for whatever it may be worth, I shall feel that I have fulfilled my task. I appeal to you as a reader to read the book as a story normally, enjoy or suffer it, but don't dissect or analyse it to extract a significance which I never intended. Tagore stated somewhere (I forget the exact words), "To know is to dissect the object of your research and destroy it." I have no right to direct your thoughts, since I am convinced that when a composition leaves my desk and assumes the printed *avatar*, it acquires an unsuspected vitality and lives a life of its own, revealing significance and meaning to a reader in which I have no part. I can only watch such results with surprise — and sometimes dismay.

The exhortation not to "dissect or analyse" his books has not been heeded: both William Walsh and Cynthia Vanden Driesen have shown the positive, helpful results of such approaches, and the latter very justly observes that "In comparison with the allusive, complex works of some of the acknowledged masters of the modern novel the novels of R.K. Narayan might not seen profoundly impressive, particularly at a cursory glance. Their simplicity, however, is more apparent than real" (63).

The essays that constitute this volume are theoretical, comparative, and exigetical; together, they provide proof of the substance that lies behind the apparent simplicity of Narayan's writing, and they amount to individual marigolds in the traditional Mysore garland of recognition and honour. Professor Mahood's address opened the conference, which celebrated Narayan's eighty-fifth birthday.

A.L. McLeod

Works Cited

Lukas, J. Anthony. "English Writing in India Declines." *New York Times,* 1 Aug. 1965: 28

Narayan, R.K. Letter. 2 Jan. 1992, to H.H. Anniah Gowda.

Vanden Driesen, Cynthia. *The Novels of R.K. Narayan.* Research Paper No. 6. Centre for South and Southeast Asian Studies. Perth : University of Western Australia, 1986.

Walsh, William. *R.K. Narayan. Writers and Their Work,* No. 224. London: British Council; Longman, 1971.

CONTENTS

1

HOMAGE TO R. K. NARAYAN

M.M. MAHOOD
(University of Kent)

Honoured as I feel at being invited to inaugurate a conference focused upon the work of R.K. Narayan, I am uneasily aware of being doubly disadvantaged for the task. First, I am a non-Indian confronting a novelist who, as V.S. Naipaul has said, writes from deep within his own society; second, I have been retired for many years from the academic scene and so remain ignorant of the responses of the latest schools of theoretical criticism to Narayan's art as a storyteller. It is patent that the very title of *The Painter of Signs* is an open invitation to the deconstructionists; that feminist criticism has great scope in the work of a writer who has said (in *My Days)* that he is "obsessed with a philosophy of woman as opposed to Man, her constant oppressor" (119); and that psychoanalytical critics can have a field day with such Oedipal tensions as that between the Financial Expert and his son Balu — one of the saddest relationships ever handled by this generally happy novelist. My preparation for the task I now face has been simply to go to my shelves, where the Malgudi books have had pride of place for many years. It follows that what I have to say cannot be a critical disquisition, but simply an act of homage, and acknowledgement made to a venerable novelist of the pleasure he has given one of his innumerable readers.

English academics tend to retire to remote villages and it is from such a setting that one comes best to appreciate the small details of Narayan's more rural stories: "Muni engaged his attention in local gossip for a few minutes, which always ended with a reference to the postmaster's wife who had eloped to the city some months before." Now it so happens that the hitherto obscure village in which I live has recently made the headlines in the British tabloid press as a result of the alleged misconduct of its parish priest with two of his women parishioners. It goes without saying that none of us villagers would dream of indulging in gossip on so sensitive a topic — yet, somehow or other, every social call ends with the guest turning back on the doorstep to ask, "By the way, have you heard anything more about the vicar?"

It is, however, all too easy to indulge in a cosy enjoyment and a facile evaluation of Narayan's stories by relating them to our own rather patronising relish for the minutiae of village or small-town life. The story "A Horse and Two Goats," from which I have just quoted, soon moves on from such gentle satire to become a penetrating study in cultural disparity as an indigent villager and a rich American tourist each pursues his thoughts about the painted clay image which the American is determined to acquire. To the stranger, the horse is envisaged as a possession, the purchase of which will enhance his social future: "We'll stand around him and have our drinks." To the man born and bred where this totally uncommunicative conversation takes place, the horse is a part of his environment, the guardian of his community, and the embodiment of its legendary past. And these values hold for the larger, more complex world of Malgudi, which, as we get to know it, proves to be so much more than a mental refuge from Western fret and hurry. There is misery in Malgudi, just as there is likely to be in any human society — one remembers the orphan body in *The Financial Expert* —but as a social world it always has the potential to be beautiful in the Schumacher sense; to be an intricate, self-sustaining organism such as James Lovelock postulates in his concept of Gaia. In Malgudi, non-human nature interpenetrates urban human existence in the form of sunlight; air; the life-bearing river; the serene tank; the great trees which, for a tree-worshipper such as myself, are a prime joy of the South Indian scene. And this capacity for sustainability and self-renewal extends through the biological into the social sphere. In *Mr. Sampath (The Printer of Malgudi)*, Srinivas perceives it as a balance of power in human relationships: "He marvelled at the invisible forces of the universe which maintained this subtle balance in all matters." In a machine, part controls part, but in the organic equipoise of a healthy community, individual adapts to individual in what Narayan terms "well-defined encounters."

For me, Narayan is the poet of such encounters, of the give and take of daily life in which, when things go right, each party makes delicate adjustments to the genetic drive that encourages us all to impose our wills on others. No other writer I know registers so exactly the egocentric impulses that keep bubbling up beneath the bonhomie of social intercourse in the form of irritation, ingratiation, boredom, sudden irrational fears, and the mental rehearsal of scenes in which we invariably take a leading and melodramatic role. The English Teacher, waiting for his wife and baby to arrive by train, wrings his hands in despair: "How was she going to get out with the child and all that luggage? The train stopped for just seven minutes. I would help her down first and then throw the things out, and if there were any boxes left over they would have to be lost with the train, that was all"(23). Needless to say, when the train does arrive, his wife calmly takes charge of the situation and neither she nor the luggage is carried on to the next station. The episode foreshadows the ultimate adjustment of personality to personality in a radiantly happy marriage, whereas the fantasies of Margayya, the Financial Expert, are doomed to be joyless in their outcome. Overhearing in the temple a father's reprimand to his son ("Don't bite your nails before God"), Margayya luxuriates in speculation about how his own son would behave in similar circumstances: " 'He'd have insisted on doing what he pleased — and not only bitten his own nails, but other people's as well'..... Margayya reflected with gratification. It seemed to be a most charming assertiveness on the part of his child" (31). This distortion of family pride, the determination to recreate his son in his own image, bodes ill for the future of the family, for Margayya is a dangerous egotist who upsets the balance of life by projecting on all round him the self-image of the great financier. Graham Greene speaks of his "innocence," but it is only possible to apply the term to this Robert Maxwell of Malgudi in the special Greene sense of an amoral and infantile self-preoccupation that disturbs the normal balance of human dealing in a way that demands the intervention of other and larger social and even transcendent forces.

It is worth saying here, in passing, that the relationship between the two novelists requires, and would be rewarding of, further study. Greene's recommendation that *Swami and Friends* should be published launched Narayan on his literary career; but his influence on Narayan, where it can be detected, is not necessarily always a happy one. Is not the ending of *The Guide* more English than Indian, the conclusion of a Greene novel rather than of one by Narayan ? The influence of the Eastern on the Western novelist remains, as far as I know, unstudied; yet the theme of *The Guide,* the con-man forced to live up to the persona he has created for himself so that in the end the mask and the man are one, is taken up by Greene and used to great effect in *The Comedians* and other books. Each novelist has crowned his long career by a brilliant excursion into pure fantasy, written as each approached his ninth decade: *A Tiger for Malgudi* in this respect is as cumulative, as quietly magisterial, as *Monsignor Quixote.* And I think an investigation into the role of the policeman in the work of each writer would be particularly revealing.

But I digress from my theme of Narayan's superb egotists, puffed up with the pride of life and demanding that all round them should dance to their tune. Jane Austen has been called merciless to egotists. Narayan, however, never raises his authorial voice to prick the bubbling self-esteem of even his most exhibitionist figures, for it is central to his faith in the underlying balance of life that such characters must in the end burn themselves out. All that is left of Mr. Sampath at the conclusion of his eponymous novel is a little red glow, and even the brutal and dangerous Vasu, the Man-Eater ends his existence in a form of spontaneous combustion. Only the monstrous circus-trainer who torments the Tiger of Malgudi is destroyed rather than allowed to dissolve; and what a satisfying moment it is when the Captain is neatly decapitated by his victim, who is surprised into the Conradian reflection that "such a flimsy character, no better than a membrane stretched over some thin framework, with so little stuff inside, should have held me in fear so long" (78).

Self-absorbed characters such as Sampath, Margayya, Vasu and Captain thus ride roughshod over the delicacy of normal relationships, which has its counterpart in the delicacy of Narayan's prose. In *My Days,* the novelist tells us that at one time he had perforce to learn a good deal about the printer's art; and the compositor's nimble and accurate selection of letter after letter and his deft insertion of each into his printing stick form fitting symbols of the novelist's own finesse in picking and placing his words: going, as he says, "to the precise phrase in the face of an experience." Perhaps it is because this precision excludes the resonances beloved of literary critics, because Narayan's narratorial voices has the unechoing clarity of a recording studio, that his writing strikes some ears as being thin and bodiless. In recent weeks I have been told by several Indian friends that this lack of resonance, together with Narayan's concentration upon the social interchanges that form the surface of daily living, result in writings that lack depth. I am inclined to associate this criticism with a similar mistrust of Shakespearean comedy which, again over the past few weeks, I have been trying to persuade audiences can be at its most profound when it is most risible. One does not have to be serious in order to be *serieux*. For in Narayan, the surface never loses touch with the depths. While some of his Indian critics thus see him as a drifting water-hyacinth, his art is perhaps better typified by the lotus, whose shining flower is anchored by a firm stem to the fertile ground beneath. And that ground, like all subsoil, is stratified — by which I mean that it is impossible to read and re-read Narayan's novels without coming to the realisation that, beneath their gentle record of mundane happenings, they carry both an anagogical and an allegorical meaning: that the events recorded, however trivial, have also a political (in the widest sense of the term) and a metaphysical significance.

Rather surprisingly, it is the anagogical dimension, the re-enactment in life's trivial pursuits of cosmic conflicts symbolised by the gods and demons of Indian mythology, which is the more accessible to the western reader. For this we can in large part thank Narayan himself, who has re-told much of that mythology in *Gods, Demons and Others* and in his subsequent adaptations from the *Ramayana* and the *Mahabharata*. These have enabled those of us who are outsiders to know a demon when we meet one — as when Vasu thrusts through Nataraj's sky-blue curtain a head composed of "powerful eyes under thick brows, a large forehead, and a shock of unkempt hair like a black halo." The terrorist who leads Sriram astray from the path of non-violence in *Waiting for the Mahatma* is no less demonic, and the Captain is surely the very Prince of Darkness. Sampath and Margayya too, though they lack essential evil, are at the mercy of demonic impulses. All these characters behave as demiurges who strive to shape an anti-world of their own devising. The Captain's parody of the real world is the significantly named Creative Circus, in which the noblest beast of the jungle is to move only as he decrees : he thrusts a stick into Raju's cage and is "greatly amused when I jumped about in pain and confusion. He said with a guffaw, 'Ah, you are a promising dancer too!' " But the master craftsman of an illusory anti-word is surely Vasu, who excels in making dead animals look as if they are alive, and who can describe as "a perfect animal" a dead elephant dispersed into bangles and umbrella stands. Even a mere demonling like Sampath parodies the divine creativity: "We will make stars if the ready-made ones are not available."

Infernal strength is opposed by the powers of light; and while in Narayan's stories the divine, as in all literary re-creations of mythology, is less easily apprehended than the demonic, the Western reader can often detect the presence of the good and the blessed in one particular motif, that of reflected light. So in *Mr. Sampath,* Srinivas pauses to wonder at a sudden, odd gleam of light in his bathroom just before the insight and understanding which flood over him as he considers his relationship with his wife, a motif repeated in the point of light caught in the belt-buckle of the policeman who puts into Srinivas's head the idea of returning to his rightful role in life as editor of *The Banner.* Most pervading of all such motifs is the lifting of the heart that comes from the reflection of sky in river or tank: a Wordsworthian experience which leads as inevitably as it does with the English poet to little nameless acts of kindness and of love.

Where Western admirers of Narayan most need help—such as I hope, this conference can provide, in discussions if not in formal papers—is in grasping the allegorical element in his stories. In a few, notably *Waiting for the Mahatma,* it is made obvious by the historical setting. But even in *The Man-Eater of Malgudi,* set so firmly in the India of Nehru's Five-Year Plans and of the Indo-Chinese War of 1962, it is surprising how, for example, the novelist's game with the notions of a bamboo and an iron curtain can be missed by normally perspicuous readers. Enlightenment would be particularly welcome about the allegorical element of *A Tiger for Malgudi.* Is it a story of the twentieth century as a whole, in which the brutality of older tyrannies has yielded place to regimes made horrific by their refinements of cruelty—a set text, as it were, for Amnesty International? Or does it have more precise, more topical, more Indian applications? I look to the papers of this conference to throw light on topics such as this for those of us who have crossed the black water to attend it. And what better setting for the attainment of such enlightenment than Mysore's Institute of Commonwealth and American Studies? For in bidding this chosen band of Narayan admirers welcome to this most agreeable of cities, I am welcoming you once more to visit Malgudi.

Works Cited

Narayan, R.K. *The English Teacher*. London : Eyre, 1945.

—, *The Financial Expert*. London: Heinemann, 1981.

—, *The Man-Eater of Malgudi*. London : Heinemann, 1962.

—, *My Days: A Memoir*. New Delhi : Orient, 1986.

2

NARRATIVE STRATEGIES IN TWO NARAYAN NOVELS

FAKRUL ALAM
(University of Dhaka)

I cannot say that I have come across more than a handful of papers devoted to Narayan's mastery of narrative techniques. It is almost as if V.S. Naipaul had the last word when he called Narayan "an instinctive, unstudied writer" (41).

No doubt Narayan himself has given credence to the widespread belief that he is a born storyteller who has no taste for complex socio-economic issues or questions of technique or form. Talking to Ved Mehta in 1962, for example, Narayan characterised himself as "an inattentive, quick writer who has little sense of style" ("Profiles" 72). Twenty years later, in another interview, he seemed to be content to leave a similar impression about his approach to fiction when he stated, "I'd be quite happy if no more is claimed for me than being just a storyteller. Only the story matters, that's all" ("only").

As if on cue from the author, many Narayan critics have gone out of their way to emphasise his simplicity and spontaneity and have eschewed formal analysis of the fiction. Reading these critics, one gets the impression that the Malgudi tales themselves and that all Narayan did was to tap the vein of storytelling in him. Perhaps this is why Ved Mehta waxed rhapsodic in 1971 about the "unpretentious, almost unliterary novels" (*John* 109).

Unwittingly, Narayan has even provided his detractors with ammunition by disclaiming technique. Thus Harsharan S. Ahluwalia is able to quote from the novelist to conclude "that most of the novels are not well-made" (61). Severely critical of what he perceives to be Narayan's decision to pander to the taste of his predominantly Western audience, Ahluwalia feels that the writer's traditional vision of life does not allow him to exhibit "that exploratory quality which gives to a creative work depth and range" (63).

So is it unnecessary to devote to Narayan's fiction the kind of analysis demanded by canonical texts? Or are we to continue the critical tradition where you cherish the storyteller but pay more attention to the telling, assuming that a writer may have his own artful ways of concealing this art? Keith Garebian is one of the handful of critics I had in mind earlier who think that most approaches to Narayan have been very superficial and that all too often the novelist's students assented to his pronouncements about his lack of technique without bothering to "establish correlations between literary form and thematic content" in the novels (70). Garebian concedes readily that Narayan's literary strategies would not place him amidst the avant-garde novelists, but he is convinced that "the novels have a sense of shape whose subtlety is sometimes revealed incrementally" (71).

This sampling of Narayan critics reveals two conflicting approaches: Narayan is seen either as a traditional storyteller for whom stories come naturally and do not have to be shaped in any way or as careful (if conservative and unspectacular) craftsman who has devised narrative strategies adequate to his distinctive view of life. But I want to go beyond the modest claims made by critics such as Garebian and talk about Narayan as a consummate artist who, at his best, displays his mastery over a wide range of narrative devices. By focussing on Narayan's handling of narrative perspective in two novels widely acknowledged as perhaps his best achievements, I want to demonstrate that he is a conscious craftsman, a novelist who believes in the concept of appropriate form, a subtle manipulator of point of view, a writer whose devices can never be taken of granted, and a master of the art fiction. The fact that *The Financial Expert* is presented by an omniscient narrator and *The Guide* alternates between first - and third-person narrator should alert us to the variety of narrative perspectives that Narayan can wield; but I hope to go beyond generalisations in displaying Narayan's control over various narrative techniques.

The Financial Expert is presented by an omniscient narrator, but as Wayne Booth has pointed out, "to say that a story is told in the first or third person, and to group novels into one or the other kind, will tell us nothing of importance unless we become more precise and describe how the particular qualities of the narrators relate to specific desired effects" (175-76). The first question to ask of the novel, then, is what Narayan is trying to say in it. One answer certainly is that the story of Margayya, the "financial expert" of the title, is about a man who pursues dubious paths to wealth, only to find out that true riches can never accrue when one turns money into a god. Margayya's obsession with money-making, his progress from a self-appointed financial expert to peasants who helps them to obtain loans from a cooperative bank to a wealthy and powerful money-lender, leads ultimately nowhere. Narayan's primary interest in Margayya is thus a moral one, for he is interested in exposing the follies and delusions of his protagonist and is intent on emphasising the transience of human action.

At this basic thematic level, then, *The Financial Expert* is a fable; we would even call it a religious fable, since Narayan's oblique reference to the ongoing quarrel between two goddesses, Lakshmi and Saraswati, indicates that you can rarely enjoy both riches and enlightenment. In other words, Margayya attains self-knowledge only when he gives up his chase of money. This seems to fall in with Naipaul's observation about Narayan's novels: "for all their delight in human oddity...they ... are less the purely social comedies... I had once taken them to be than religious books" (22).

It seems to me, however, that *The Financial Expert* is more than a social comedy and not just a religious fable. In fact, I find in the novel what Naipaul says he did not detect in Narayan's fiction: "the distress of India", "the cruel and overwhelming" reality of the life of a section of its people, and record of "dereliction and smallness" (21). I am struck, for instance, by the critique Narayan directs at the way things were in India in the thirties and the forties : corruption and red-tapism of financial institutions such as the cooperative and the high-handedness of their officials; the crippling dowry system and the endless litigation that drove people to lending money; the venality of the clergy; the endless humiliations suffered by everyman and the marginalisation of women; the opportunism and the cynicism of businessmen and officials in wartime India,[1] and the activities of touts, money-lenders, and hustlers of various stripes who flourish in financial jungles. *The*

Financial Expert may be a religious fable about the pointlessness of a life solely devoted to hoarding money without attaining true enlightenment, but just as Bunyan's *Vanity Fair* is rooted in a real world of urban deceit Narayan's narrative draws strength from his concrete presentation of the struggle for existence in Margayya's world.

Most of Margayya's life, indeed, has been a matter of devising ways and means of surviving. If you fail to be predatory in this world, you are liable to disappear in the maws of society. It is a world with its own pecking order : Margayya is cunning and a bully with his clients outside the cooperative, but he feels at this stage of his career "that the world treated him with contempt because he had no money" (14). Aggressive and unfeeling in dealing with country bumpkins, he is actually insecure about his own position in society and full of self-pity. Thus "somebody driving by in a car of the latest model seemed to look at him for a fleeting second and Margayya fancied that he caught a glimpse of contempt in his eyes" (20). If he is obsessive about money in life, how perilous his position in society is : "It seemed such a formidable and horrible world that he wondered how he had managed to exist at all," he thinks at one point (77). Inheriting almost nothing, and with very little education, he must fend for himself with his wits all the time.

Narayan's objective in devising a narrative strategy for *The Financial Expert* therefore was to come up with a perspective which would allow him to give his work a fable-like quality but would also enable him to reflect the intensities of everyday life as experienced by an essentially vulnerable man. Narayan meets his objective splendidly by giving his novel the kind of omniscient narrator associated with fables and traditional storytelling while *focalising* most of the story through Margayya.[2] To put it somewhat differently, Narayan takes full advantage of the infinite flexibility enjoyed by an omniscient narrator while retaining many of the privileges of the first-person narrator.

In fact, it is not an exaggeration to say that Narayan has achieved in *The Financial Expert* almost complete impersonalised dramatic projection, at least as James Joyce defined this technique in *A Portrait of the Artist as a Young Man:* "The personality of the artist passes into the narration itself, flowing round and round the persons like a vital sea....The artist, like the God of creation, remains within of behind or beyond or above his handiwork, invisible, refined out of existence" (214-15).[3] To this end, Narayan cuts down on summary, emphasises scenes and prefers not to come between the narrative and the reader, his objective being to present events dramatically, so that a sense of immediacy is created and we get personally involved in Margayya's story.

Narayan, of course, has not completely eliminated summary or dispensed with contextualising comments; from time to time he will offer descriptions of the background or information about Margayya's life before the narrative began or in periods within the story time but not covered in the novel. Nevertheless, even on these occasions Narayan attempts to involve readers in the action, providing those details which enable them to "watch him in his setting a little more closely" (1). Moreover, we see Margayya from the perspective of clients, or neighbours, or relatives-cases—Genette would say of *external focalisation*. For instance, when Margayya has begun to run out of space for the cash he had been amassing in the last phase of his career, and just before his fall, his brother's wife, who has been straining her ears against a small crack in the wall that divided the two brothers, hears Margayya say to his wife, "you will have to clear out of the upstairs room too'" (201).

I will concede, though, that while these attempts to involve the reader in Margayya's story through the people who know him best are interesting, there is nothing remarkable about them technically — Narayan is simply adopting in them the narrative strategy utilised by storytellers of all ages. What is impressive, however, is Narayan's bid to get readers involved in Margayya's life by taking them into his mind, thereby ensuring sympathy for the man and understanding of his often disagreeable actions. The technique involved is that of what Genette calls *internal focalisation,* but I really am talking here about a variety of devices through which we are given access to a character's inner life. One such device that Narayan uses frequently is that of free indirect speech, a technique which Shlomith Rimman-Kenan describes as a combination of the "narrator's voice and a character's pre-verbal perception or feeling" (111). For example, when Arul Doss, the head peon of the cooperative bank, looms as a menace in Margayya's angle of vision, the narrative switches from omniscient narration ("He [Margayya] had a busy day...") to free indirect speech: "What right had he [Arul Doss] to insult or browbeat him? What had he done that they themselves did not do?" (17).

Quite often in *The Financial Expert* the narrative takes an even more inward turn until we have something resembling the interior monologue or stream-of-consciousness technique employed in the novels of high modernism, albeit in a more rudimentary form. One example of this will suffice, and it is from a passage where Margayya, on a quest for a lotus prescribed as a means to attaining riches by a cryptic priest who has also asked him to recite certain prayers, encounters Dr. Pal, a con-man and author of a semi-pornographic work that he hopes to pass off as a contribution to sociology. He shows his manuscript to Margayya, who eventually will get to publish it and will get his first real financial break in life through it. As he returns home from his meeting with Dr. Pal, Margayya's mind is in ferment as he thinks about this strange man, his book, the priest's injunction, and his own future:

> This man wanted to put in pictures — what a wicked fellow.
> It'd be most awkward....Why was Dr. Pal interested in the
> subject [of sexual relations]? Must be an awful rake...if he
> could write all that and was unmarried.... Some of the chapter
> headings came to his mind. He realised with a shock what line
> his thoughts were pursuing, and he pulled them back to the
> *verse;* the priest had told him to let his mind rest fully on its
> meaning while repeating it. He kept saying: "Oh Goddess,
> who affordest...." etc., and unknown to him his thoughts slipped
> out and romped about — chiefly about the fruits of the
> penance he was undertaking: forty days of this afterwards. He
> visualised his future. How was wealth going to flow in? When
> he became rich, suppose he bought from his brother the next
> house too.... (70)

In this passage, and there are quite a few like it in the novel, Narayan skilfully blends third-person narration ("He realised..."), free indirect discourse ("How was wealth going to flow in ?"), direct discourse ("He kept saying :'O Goddess..."), and ellipsis and employs an accelerated narrative pace and frequent switches between the past (what the priest said, and Dr. Pal and his book), the present (focussing on the prayer), and the future ("When he became rich, suppose..."), to create the illusion of having access to the mind of a man whose "thoughts slipped out and romped about." It seems clear that Narayan's goal in such passages is to capture the flow of Margayya's mental process and to stimulate the mixture of memories, expectations, feelings, obligations, and random associations that constitute our waking consciousness.

Because we are thus continually led into Margayya's mind, we get to realise how intensely he reacts to a life of deprivation and how much he wants to rise above his circumstances. Narayan's technique also makes us aware of the real emotions Margayya goes through as well as the mask he puts on for the everyday world, thereby ensuring tolerance for his follies. But Margayya is not the only character we come to understand and care about, because Narayan's narrative method takes us into his consciousness; nor is he the only focaliser in the novel. His wife, Meenakshi (for most of the novel a figure in the background of the action, occupying the place reserved for women in Margayya's world) comes into her own towards the end of the novel when Nargayya's provides his variant of the interior monologue for her too. The moment when we enter her consciousness is when she is reacting to a quarrel between her husband and her son. Her son's gruff manners make her think for a moment that he has inherited them from her father. But then she thinks of the way her son has been smoking lately and realises that he has picked up such a bad habit because Margayya has given him too much money and too little guidance. This leads her to think about the way her husband has changed as he became rich — he has been treating her even more brusquely than before. But she feels that she is powerless to do anything to change father or son or stop them quarreling. All she can do is watch with "resignation and fear, "knowing that "the best way to attain some peace of mind in life" for someone in her position "was to maintain silence" (137). As a result, "she watched the trouble brewing between the two as if it all happened behind a glass screen" (138). Pretty soon the son is in tears and the father close to crying, but the point of view now switches to Margayya. He felt "his eyes smarting with tears and felt ashamed of it before his son and that stony-faced woman who stood at the doorway of the kitchen and relentlessly watched" (138). However, because we have had access to Meenakshi's mind a moment back, we know that the "stony-faced woman" is going through some strong emotions, that her silence is pregnant with the unspoken accusations of a wife against her husband, and that her stare is a goad on Margayya's conscience; he knows that in his obsession with money he has ruined their chance of domestic happiness. Here, as elsewhere in *The Financial Expert*, Narayan's narrator moves deftly in and out of the minds of his character, testifying to the skill with which Narayan manipulates narrative perspective and utilises technique to further his thematic concerns.

But so quietly does Narayan slip from one perspective to another, and so seldom does the narrator draw attention to himself, that we are content to attend to the narrative without paying much attention to the strategy employed to present Margayya's story. This is also true of Narayan's handling of time in the novel, for even though he is not averse to utilising devices such as flashbacks and flashforwards to arouse our sympathies for his at times disagreeable protagonist, we tend not to detect the disruptions made in the chronological order of the story. I will give one example of each device from *The Financial Expert*. There is a good example of the use of the flashback when Margayya is suddenly griefstruck at the report of his son's death. He remembers then the pledge he had made to the gods and the pilgrimage he and his wife had undertaken when she was having problems conceiving. As we enter Margayya's mind, we realise that he is connecting the present sad event with the happy memory of the quest. But it is the irrelevance of the details of the pilgrimage to his current situation that is striking. He remembers, for example, how he "had clutched a brightly-polished pot and, followed by his saffron-clad wife, had gone from door to door.... He suddenly recollected now how amused he had felt when he saw his face in that burnished pot" (161). However, throughout these moments of retrospection when he is escaping into a prelapsarian world, Margayya remains incorrigibly himself; that is, a man obsessed with wealth. Thus he remembers, too, how he had redeemed not a moment too soon his pledge to the gods to offer to them silver rupees equivalent to the weight of a child if they granted him this boon, for when the child was eventually born, "he showed a tendency to grow heavier each day" (161).

Margayya, of course, discovers later that his son is still alive, and the flashforward device is used when he meets his son again. Balu had actually run away and was working as an odd-job boy in a movie hall, and Margayya finds him there in a dirty and dishevelled state. This is the moment when the narrative takes a leap forward in time : "As he later explained to his relations, the moment he saw him he felt as if he had swallowed a live cinder" (173). As in his use of the flashback, Narayan is disrupting the chronological order thus to humanise his protagonist and to keep us involved in his lifestory and acquaint us with his thought-processes. Typically, though, so unobtrusive is Narayan's narrative strategy that we hardly ever think of complimenting his handling of perspective or order in such scenes.

But if Narayan's manipulation of narrative perspective and order in *The Financial Expert* is so subtle as to escape notice, *The Guide* is a novel where the narrative strategy continually draws attention to itself. This is because in presenting the story of Raju, a scamp who ends up being perceived as a saint by a lot of people, Narayan uses both first-person and third-person narration and a braided time-scheme. When we first meet Raju, for example, he is seen from the perspective of the omniscient narrator. He has just got out of jail then and has ended up in an abandoned place where he has found an admirer in Velan, a man from a neighboring village. Soon after the two meet, Raju and the narrator take turns in telling the story of Raju's passage from the world of innocence to the world of experience. While Raju relates to Velan his progress from a wide-eyed child to the owner of a railway stall to tourist guide to the lover and impresario of the classical dancer Rosie to jailbird, the narrator punctuates Raju's narrative by showing his dealings with Velan and the villagers who embrace him as a spiritual guide who will lead the village out of a drought through a penitential fast. Raju's purpose in telling his story to Velan is to demystify the latter about his spiritual powers and to emphasise his shady past; Velan, however, is unmoved by the story and continues to see him as a guru. After Raju concludes his narrative, the omniscient narrator takes sole charge of the narrative duties. He then concludes it, showing us a Raju who may or may not be at the point of achieving transcendence.

So why does Narayan utilise a braided time-scheme, oscillating points of view, and an open-ended conclusion for *The Guide?* Certainly, these are devices alien to the kind of storytelling tradition that Narayan has placed himself in. Moreover, it seems reasonable to assume — especially after our analysis of the narrative strategy of *The Financial Expert* — that the writer must have deliberated at great length on the combinations and variations of angles that would most effectively project Raju's life for readers before hitting on the right mix of narrative devices to be employed. In fact, Narayan indicated clearly at one point in *The Guide* that he is quite aware that a chronological narrative is not always the natural mode of storytelling. Raju, who has nothing of the artist in him and sees Rosie first as someone to possess sexually and later as a means of getting money, demands a "chronological narration" from her when he hears from her that her husband had deserted her because of her infidelity. Rosie, a true artist and a complex woman, is unable to provide such narrative and keeps "swinging forward and backward and talking in scraps" so that he gets her story "all in a knot" (128-29).

In other words, when complicated human emotions are involved, a linear narrative or a clear perspective or a neat conclusion will not always do. That may be one reason why Narayan chooses an unusual narrative strategy for *The Guide*. Another is suggested by Keith Garebian who, as I have stressed before, is a critic who has something worthwhile to say about Narayan's mastery of the art of fiction. In "Strategy and Theme in the Art of R.K. Narayan," Garebian notes the "frequent interruptions, pauses, and breaks in the narrative" and finds these disruptions to "accord well with Raju's agitation and changes in identity" (74).

In his pages on the narrative strategy deployed in *The Guide*, Garebian chooses to concentrate on Narayan's manipulation of tempo cross-cuts between different perspectives or the effects he achieves by juxtaposing third-person narration with first-person narration. To take one example from the first part of the novel, the story of Devaka, "a man of ancient times who begged for alms at the temple gate every day and would not use any of his collections without first putting them at the feet of the god" (15), comes up twice in the novel: first in the narrator's account of one encounter between Raju and Velan, where Raju is using the story as an *exemplum* to display his wisdom, and immediately afterwards in Raju's own narrative about his childhood when he recounts how the story was told to him by his mother to put him to sleep. In the narrator's account, we are told that Raju could not complete the story because halfway through it "he could not remember either its course or its purport" (15), but we need to listen to Raju's narrative a little later to realise that he had to lapse into silence as an adult before Velan because he would always go to sleep before his mother could even go through the preamble of the story when he was a child. All that the mature Raju remembers about Devaka is that "he was a hero, saint, or something of the kind" (17), a point that has ironic implications about his own status at the end of the novel, where the reader has to decide if Raju has assumed sainthood or just lost consciousness because of hunger and fatigue. But there is irony also in the narrator's account of Raju's failure to complete the Devaka *exemplum* to Velan; Velan is not bothered by Raju's lapse as a storyteller, for "He was of the stuff disciples are made of; an unfinished story or an incomplete moral never bothered him; it was all in the scheme of life" (15). Here, or later in the novel, Raju can do no wrong as far as Velan and the villagers are concerned; faced with their unshakeable belief in his commitment to them and in his mystic power, he will have no option except to fast till his consciousness ebbs away.

The narrator's comment on Velan's attitude to unfinished stories or incomplete morals raises a very interesting question: is Narayan using it to prepare us for the ending he provides for *The Guide*? In other words, is the conclusion of the novel, where Raju may or may not be at the point of achieving transcendence, deliberately left open-ended by Narayan because "it was all in the scheme of life"? To vary the question somewhat, is the narrator being ironic about Raju's final gesture as he sinks into the river while telling Velan that he can feel the rains coming, or are we to accept this as proof that Raju has finally achieved the power to work miracles through his self-sacrifice?

While it will be impossible to answer these questions with finality, one way to tackle them is through a study of Narayan's control of distance in the novel, distance being used here to mean the "variations in the amount of detail and consciousness presented, in the range between intricacy and remoteness" (Martin 124). In the first part of *The Guide*, where the narrator follows Raju after his release from prison and tracks him as he begins to play the part of a guru for Velan, we are placed at a remove from Raju and don't have much of an access to his consciousness. As a result, we watch with amusement and skepticism as Raju puts on the mask of a spiritual guide. But as the mature Raju takes increasing control of the narrative chores from the omniscient narrator in the middle part of the novel, we get more insights into the psychology of the man; in the process the distance between him and us is reduced. By the middle of *The Guide*, in fact, we have begun to live Raju's thoughts. Even in the few sections devoted to third-person narration, we are placed closer to his consciousness than before and can hear him thinking. Thus, when the villagers air their gratitude to him for fasting for them, the omniscient narrator articulates Raju's bewildered response: "Their babble was confusing. But their devotion to him was unquestionable. There was so much warmth in their approach...." (93). In the first-person narrative too, the mature Raju who is relating the story of his flawed life to Velan seems intent on presenting events as they unfolded to his younger, erring self. For example, the older Raju enacts "the abnormal frame of mind" he was in many years ago when he was with Rosie: "I was losing a great deal of my mental relaxation. I was obsessed with the thoughts of Rosie. I revelled in memories of the hours I had spent with her last or in anticipation of what I'd be doing next. I had several problems to contend with. Her husband was the least of them" (101). The short, choppy sentences here simulate the agitated mind of Raju the lover; surely the narrative here is as close as it can be to the central character's experiencing self.

By the end of the novel, though, and after Raju has terminated his narrative, the distance between us and Raju begins to increase again till we can once more view the things happening to him with detachment and irony. Events are now presented not only from his perspective but also from that of a wandering newspaper correspondent, James J. Malone, an American film producer attracted to the story of Raju's fast, and the villagers. Narayan tries to capture in his prose the carnivalesque air of the village where a saint appears to be embracing sainthood: an interview of Raju as Swami (taken by Malone), a doctor's report, and a "top-priority government telegram" (220) manifest the comic vision and manic energy at work in the final pages. In such a context, Raju's last act, where he "sags" down into the river like a "baby" while talking about the rains that he can feel coming, does not appear to be something that we can take in without suppressing a smile. Indeed, we are at a sufficient distance from him throughout the last chapter to see Raju's "sacrifice" ironically and perhaps even cynically. It may be in the nature of things for villagers like Velan to apotheosise Raju-types, but the narrative mode of the novel directs readers to draw their own skeptical and independent conclusion from the unfinished story.

The fact that *The Guide* is an open-ended work points to another aspect of the often complex narrative strategies that underlie Narayan's always simple-seeming novels: he expects his readers to do more work in interpreting his fiction than does the traditional storyteller. Indeed, it is not too fanciful to conclude from *The Guide* that Narayan expected his readers to complete the meaning of the novel and would not have been surprised if they had taken it away from him. This, at least, is one of the things I deduce from Velan's response to Raju's narration. Raju tells his story to convince Velan that he is no saint who can save the villagers from the drought by fasting; Velan, nevertheless, resists this conclusion and thereby seals Raju's fate. The narratee thus determines the outcome of the narrative by rejecting the intentions of the narrator. And even though Velan is obviously wrong about Raju, he does help to illustrate the autonomy readers can enjoy in any given narrator-communication situation: the narrator may present his story, but readers can and often will make what they want to do with it. As Genette puts it in *Narrative Discourse:* "we should not confuse the *information* given by a focalised narrative with the *interpretation* the reader is called on to give of it (or that he gives without being invited to)" (197).

My reconsideration of the narrative strategies employed by Narayan has, I hope, proved the following: that he is not "an instinctive, unstudied writer" but a careful craftsman who chooses the narrative techniques which will convey his themes best; that he is not "a traditional storyteller" (if by that phrase we mean someone who uses narrative formulas and devices which are unsophisticated); that he is not afraid of experimenting with narrative perspectives, time schemes, and different levels and voices of narration; and that he is not necessarily or merely rewriting religious myths and reaffirming spiritual themes belonging to what Naipaul called "an intensely Hindu" world, but a complex man, sensitive to socio-economic problems, skeptical of age-old routes to sanctification, and even quietly subversive of the established moral order and the notion that we must accept our lot. To put the case for Narayan positively: he is a writer whose exploratory nature helps to give each of his novels a certain depth and range. I hope that this paper will help stop forever talk about his artlessness and plainness. There are many questions to be asked and many roads to be taken. I wonder, for example, if we can get access to his working notes or drafts, for that would confirm the premise on which this paper was based: R.K. Narayan is a major novelist who has, as Yeats put it in another context so long ago, laboured "to be beautiful."

Notes

1. In a remarkable paragraph of Part Four of the novel (pp. 192-93), Narayan instances in clinical fashion the corrupt and unlawful paths to wealth being pursued in India during the Second World War.

2. I make the distinction here between point of view and focalisation first made by Gerard Genette in *Narrative Discourse.* Genette emphasises that in talking about narrative perspective we really need to raise two questions: "who is the character whose point of view orients the narrative perspective? and the very different question, who is the narrator? — or, more simply, the question who sees? and the question who speaks?" We need, therefore, to distinguish between focaliser and narrator in some instances. In other words, *The*

Financial Expert has an omniscient narrator but most of the novel is focalised through Margayya.

3. Almost, but not quite. There are a few instances in the novel where the author speaks out in his own voice. See the generalisations on p. 99 and p. 162 for instances of authorial intrusions in the narrative.

Works Cited

Ahluwalia, Harsharan S. "Narayan's Sense of Audience." *Ariel* 15: 1 (Jan. 1986): 59-65.

Alam, Fakrul. "Plot and Character in Narayan's *The Man-Eater of Malgudi:* A Reassessment." *Ariel* 19:3 (July 1988): 77-92.

Booth, Wayne. "Distance and Point-of-View: An Essay in Classification." *The Novel: Modern Essays in Criticism.* Ed. Robert M. Davis. Englewood Cliffs, NJ: Prentice, 1969.

Garebian, Keith. "Strategy and Theme in the Art of R.K. Narayan." *Ariel* 5:4 (Oct. 1979): 70-81.

Genette, Gerard. *Narrative Discourse.* Trans. Jane E. Lewin. Oxford: Blackwell, 1980.

Joyce, James. *A Portrait of the Artist as a Young Man,* 1916. Harmondsworth: Penguin, 1960.

Martin, Wallace. *Recent Theories of Narrative.* Ithaca, NY: Cornell UP, 1986.

Mehta, Ved. "Profiles: The Train Had Just Arrived at Malgudi Station." *New Yorker* 38: 30 (15 Sep. 1962): 57-74. —. *John is Easy to Place.* Harmondsworth: Penguin, 1971.

Narayan, R.K. *The Financial Expert.* 1952. Chicago: U of Chicago P. 1981.

—, *The Guide.* 1958. London: Penguin, 1988.

—, "'Only the Story Matters': An Interview." *India Today* 7:3 (1-15 Feb. 1982): 61.

Naipaul, V.S. *India: A Wounded Civilization.* London: Penguin, 1979.

Rimmon-Kenan, Shlomith. *Narrative Fiction: Contemporary Poetics.* London: Methuen, 1983.

3

THE DIALECTICS OF MYTH AND IRONY IN R. K. NARAYAN

K. CHELLAPPAN
(Bharathidasan University)

In his *R.K. Narayan: A Critical Appreciation,* Professor William Walsh writes, "The new mind requires the new voice, and the new voice is discovered by the writer's genius for intimately registering the idiom of his own world" (1). The new voice that Walsh recognised in the work produced in Indian in the nineteenth and twentieth centuries can be heard most authentically in the novels of R.K. Narayan. But a really new voice can be based only on something really old — and in the art of R.K. Narayan we find a synthesis of the realism of the West with the mythic imagination of the East.

His novels may be called mythical comedies or modern fables in so far as they portray the absurdities and the incongruities of life in modern Indian society in a fictional mode that is simultaneously fabulistic and ironic. They portray a two-tiered reality in which there is an intersection of modern time with mythical time, and their sense of comedy arises out of an interplay of a Western sense of comedy and a mythical sense of life as *lila.* According to Margaret Berry, "Phenomena are for him but Maya, Prakrits, glancings gleanings, refractions — myriad as they are — from an eternal static Brahman holding infinite for ever unrealized potential. The world is, accordingly, not to be taken *ultimately* as more serious or important than the shadows of the forest or white caps on the waves" ("Narayan" 1). And this mythic sense of life as an illusion dovetails into the Western sense of life as a comedy in the art of Narayan. M.K. Naik says that Mulk Raj Anand usually deals with "what man has made of man," Raja Rao with what man should make of God (or a force larger than himself), and R.K. Narayan with the quintessential irony of what man can make of himself and of the entire business of living (3). He adds :

> The distinct development that his work shows over more than forty years from his first novel, *Swami and Friends* (1935), to .... *The Painter of Signs* (1976) is mainly in the direction of his employment of irony in portraying character and relationship ... a giant leap from irony as weapon to irony as vision, from irony of brief moment to irony of the great occasion, from ironic filigree to ironic architectonics, from intermittent irony to integral irony, from local irony arising desultorily out of amused superior insight to universal irony informing the entire action as a total serio-comic vision of man's fate. (77)

Ron Shepherd sees "an architectural duality in which modernity super-imposes on tradition" and irony as inverted allegory; he adds that in the novels of Narayan, irony begins where allegory ends. But we would like to emphasise the persistent and persuasive dialectics of the mythical and the ironic modes in Narayan's art.

The synthesis of myth and irony can be seen in Malgudi itself, which seems to be a microuniverse or symbol of the cosmic-comic spirit generating relationships in which there is a sudden explosion of routine existence into some sort of temporary significance, the very brevity being part of the significance. The towering ego of the puny individual seems to be incongruously juxtaposed with the beautiful and permanent forms of nature. In this inverted or comic Wessex, we see the inflated ego temporarily disturb the rhythm of the cosmic poise and set its own rhythm. At another level, the distant hills and the River Sarayu might be taken to symbolise permanence and flow respectively — and also their interdependence — the very flow of the Sarayu emanating from the partaking of the permanence of the hills. Against the poise of the non-human world is seen the flux of the human comedy. Only a few aspects of nature are made to intervene now and then in crucial moments of the plot, quietly reminding us of their existence, their appearance in such moments signifying both continuity and development, stability and flow. From this point of view, the plot seems to be an imposition of the human pattern over the cosmic, a ripple in the cosmic poise or even a deviation from the norm. The great

permanence is always there — but man is conscious of it only now and
then. But from another point of view (i.e., the stories) cosmic seems to
interrupt the human, and it is made a mute spectator, quietly accompanying
the human drama. Here is the quintessence of the comedy : the cosmic
is reduced to the human proportion and perspective whereas man pretends
to be cosmic. This exaggerated human gesture could either be tragic or
comic — or, as in most cases of Narayan heroes, tragi-comic.

The socio-ethical life portrayed in the novels of Narayan is rooted
in the ageless past of India, of which the myths are the objective
correlative. The characters are allegoric reductions, as they are reduced
to a role of a particular character. But the particular becomes the
universal; the part signifies the whole — the hero himself, mostly an
isolated individual, becomes the only member of a class — *the* bachelor
of Arts, *the* financial expert, *the* vendor of sweets, for example. The
generic use of the definite article both specifies and universalises the
character. The definite article can also be justified in the sense that the
character is part of an environment shared by us and the character, who
is reduced to a quality or profession; he is also extended in the sense
of being representative of men in a particular aspect. The "obsession"
and the "impostor component" of these characters would relate them
to the archetypes of Northrop Frye.

If the characters are mythical or allegoric in their universal or
ethical dimension, there is irony because of the tension between the
ethical and the human, between the dharmic role and the human.
Another dimension of the titles closely connected with this is worth
mentioning here: up to a point, there is a comic confusion or tug-of-
war between the literal and the metaphoric senses (the physical and the
spiritual), particularly, in *The Financial Expert* with Margayya showing
the way to fetch money. Even the English teacher gives up teaching at
the end. The guide is guided by others — and from being a guide in
the literal sense, evolves into a guide in the spiritual sense, though
unwillingly and unwittingly too: he literally explodes into the mythical.
In *The Vendor of Sweets* there is not only the irony of the vendor of
sweets advising the others to conquer taste, but also there is the other
contradiction of his inability to conquer attachment, while always talking
of the Gita.

The enticing attraction of life is reduced to Jiloby, but that also
evolves into a symbol. Even though there is not so much irony or
symbolism in *The Painter of Signs* , in this case also, in the beginning,

everything is reduced to being organic or symbolic, and in the final phase Raman discovers that the only identity that is real and left of him is that of the painter of signs.

All these titles seem to suggest that in life what matters is to play a role and become it— which is like the fulfilment of one's dharma. Though there is a discrepancy between the role assigned to you and the role that you are playing, that is the essence of the human comedy: it does not deny you the possibility of becoming the role and thereby transcending it. The comedy arises out of the violation of the dharma; but that is only an illusion, and everything returns to equilibrium, just as the self of the characters has an illusory active manifestation and a deep static core.

Man reduced to an aspect, but symbolising all his human potentials, becomes the archetype of Man in particular aspect. In this sense, his protagonists are comparable to humours; but in Narayan, this approach elevates his comedies into myths— the central myth being the comedy of being human. The reduced individual becomes a mythic prototype: metonymy explodes into myth and allegory; conversely, myths and allegory are reduced to the ironic perspective.

Mr. Sampath (The Printer of Malgudi), which marks the beginning of Narayan's mature art, centres in a traditional tale of the burning of Kama: two of the story's central characters, Ravi and Mr. Sampath, become hopelessly infatuated with a beautiful star who is playing the role of the temptress in a modern film version of the story of Kama. There is not the ironic parallel (or parody) of myth and modern reality, but they merge into each other, and this makes the story more comic. "When a dispute develops between the main male actor who is playing Shiva and the film's producer, who is Sampath, Shiva descends from Kailas, angry and demanding his salary. Sampath, who is also infatuated with the Temptress, decides to take this man's place and ironically dons the mask of sexual restraint," writers Ron Shepherd, who comments that this "has the effect of affirming the connecting link between two different sorts of reality, that of mythology and tradition and that of actuality and modern everyday life" (80).

The "connection" or the "confusion" of art and reality is also symbolic of the connection or confusion of myth and contemporary reality. The myth is itself made ironic because of the intrusion of reality upon art or the total identification of art and reality. In one episode, before they could see where it originated, Ravi was seen whizzing past the others like a bullet, knocking down the people in his way...rushing between Shiva's extended arms and Parvathi, and knocking Shiva aside with such violence that he fell amidst his foliage in Kailas in a most ungodly manner. Next minute they saw Parvathi struggling in the arms of Ravi, who was trying to kiss her on her lips and carry her off. (189)

Commenting on this, Margaret Berry says that in Leoncavallo's opera *I Pagliacci,* real life erupts into the opera (as is also the case with *Hamlet)*, whereas in *Mr. Sampath* the eternal paradigms intrude into the world of maya; she also refers to Parvathi's divinity being displayed as false in the play, whereas what is false in the play is taken for real ("Ramayana" 61).

Though Margaret Berry is alive to the link between the mythical and the contemporary and has traced several mythical roles underlying the characters of Sampath, Ravi and Shanthi, she sees the mythic as subsuming the ironic, whereas we would like to see they mythical itself penetrated by the ironic vision. The unreal world of art is also a metaphor for reality, and illusion and reality seem to exchange places, as in *Hamlet.* Sampath also dances to his destruction — and to his salvation, as it happens, for on the heels of catastrophe come illumination and revelation. There is a subtle relationship between the tandava dance of Shiva, in which the angry god beats out wild rhythm that destroys the world at the end of the cycle, and Sampath's dance, which makes not only the myth illuminate the contemporary disorder but also establishes a deeper link between the two. This is done precisely by a comic or ironic rendering of myth itself.

The Financial Expert is fundamentally an ironic fable with mythic undertones. Margayya's rise and fall in the contemporary financial world is ironically linked with the worship of the goddess Lakshmi, and there is the comic juxtaposition of the Central Cooperative Land Mortgage Bank and the deserted garden where Margayya searches for the lotus. The belief system embodied in the myth of the goddess Lakshmi is very much alive in the contemporary Indian consciousness, but the way in which Narayan makes his character indulge in rituals for acquiring wealth makes it very comic. The spiritual is confused with the secular, and Margayya's religious faith is wrongly and comically placed, writes Walsh, on "so secular an object as a work on the sociology of sex, and by so non-religious a figure as Dr. Pal" (79). There is some link between Margayya's worship and his acquisition of wealth, but there is also an equally miraculous loss of wealth. Though there is no logical or causal link between action and consequence, the moral order asserts itself, and the novel ends with Margayya's return to the original spot.

It is in *The Guide* that we find a greater interplay of myth and irony. The myth of Shiva and the Ganges, though not explicit, is the prototype underlying this story of a sinner-saint who, by the working of a moral force larger than himself and to which he slowly submits, becomes a martyr and brings rains to the village in the very process of seeking shelter and basic things for himself. The metaphysical notion of life as an illusion and action as mere acting find the fullest fictional rendering in this novel. Raju, the ex-jailbird, has always been a great role-player, and in this novel (which is an inverted myth), acting becomes an archetypal image — because all the time there is a comic discrepancy between the man and the mask; finally, the man becomes the mark. Raju becomes more and more an amused spectator of himself; but at the same time, there is a stripping of the external layers, which brings him closer to the truth of his being. The negative core of being is given reality by the illusion of others; later, he imparts reality to the illusion of others by his willed action.

The passive sufferer becomes the true actor, and here we have another Indian notion of karma becoming character; but here karma is one's own deeds in the immediate past and now. Irony becomes both a structural principle and a source of moral discovery, since every action is pregnant with a meaning beyond the intention of the participants, and the process of making of a saint is sublime and ridiculous as he remains disturbingly human till the very end. But the irony is deeper, because he becomes a collaborator only in the process of his discovery of his true identity — though in the negative way. This Shiva is an embodiment of Dionysian energy and appetite for life; but like Shiva again, there is the ascetic in him — though he accepts that role unwillingly, which makes it also human. Rosie is his Parvathi, and right in the beginning he reveals a capacity to go beyond the self in his reaction to the dance. "I could honestly declare that while I watched her perform, my mind was free, for once, from all carnal thoughts. I viewed her as a pure abstraction. She could make me forget my surroundings" (110). She identifies herself with the dance and attains impersonality through art, whereas Raju first thinks that he is the force behind the dance and only finally realises that it is the self that moves with the dance. She, like Shanthi of *Mr Sampath,* is also linked with the cobra, which is a symbol of primordial energy; but her dance lifts "the cobra out of its class of an underground reptile into a creature of grace and divinity and the ornaments of Gods" (151). The whole scene is reminiscent of *Mr. Sampath* and suggests a link between the stage and the world.

In *The Man-Eater of Malgudi,* myth is more explicit — now the myth of Pamasura, of evil destroying itself, brought out through a modern Rakshasha; and Sastri, one of the characters, refers to the parallel. Structurally, too, we have the juxtaposition of the story with the enactment of that old myth; in fact, the story *is* the enactment of the myth. Vasu, M.A., the taxidermist, bursts upon the peaceful, rhythmic life of Nataraj, the painter. (The names and the professions are significant.) There is a symmetrical and sustained contrast between his way and that of Nataraj: he becomes a threat to all the organic values by his relentless pursuit of destruction as a passion which, by a relentless logic, ends with his own destruction — again by his own hand — trying to destroy mosquitoes. Rangi is his Mohini, but again there is no direct correlation between any human effort to destroy him and his end. As Naik puts it, "Vasu is destroyed not so much by Rangi as through her" (10). He also refers to the link between Rangi and Mohini, but in Narayan the parallel is always ironic, because Rangi, unlike Mohini, is a poor dancer whose morals are suspect. But this is part of Narayan's technique of bringing the myth down to the dusty earth. The universal war between good and evil is brought out in this story of two familiar human beings; and in this modern fable, too, the sublime evil is brought out as sheer absurdity.

The link between *The Vendor of Sweets* and the Chandrapida story is obvious. G.S. Amur has referred to Bana's *Kadambari,* which speaks of the lake Achhoda ("clear water") at the foot of the Kailasa mountain in the heart of a forest and the Shiva temple built on its northern bank, which provide the setting for Mahashveta's encounter with Pundarika and also for Chandrapida's chance discovery of her, which leads to his union with Kadambari (97). In *The Vendor of Sweets,* Jagan's initiation is related to the garden on the other bank of the Saraju, the temple, and a lotus pond. When Jagan is on the road to illumination (or another "Janma"), we are told of "the pond with the blue lotus" in a still environment, which signifies the awakening of the soul and its still music. Then there is the symbolic descending of the moss-covered steps, watching (with fascination) bees swarming on the blue lotus. But even on the threshold of this new awareness or birth, Narayan is not blind to the comedy. "If I do not perish in this water, I shall perish of pneumonia. In my next life I'd like to be born...." His mind runs through various choices. Pet dog? Predatory cat? Street-corner donkey? Maharajah on an elephant? Anything but a moneymaking sweet-market with a spoilt son. According to Amur, the presentation of the symbol in *The Financial Expert* is ironic, while in *The Vendor of Sweets* it moves from irony to affirmation. But the irony is here also, and Jagan's epiphany takes place when he dozes off at the foot of the statue. He is linked with Buddha at the end: "He still had to pay his visit to his house, to collect a few things he needed, though he would prefer to walk off, just walk, as the Buddha did when he got enlightenment." But immediately we are brought back to the human time: "It was five o'clock, his usual hour for the back for half a century" and the human weakness, "the very sunlight, the cold bath and the gruel had mitigated somewhat the ardour of his renunciation" (183).

In *The Painter of Signs* we have a modern version of the Sandhanu story of the *Mahabharata:* here, Daisy of the Family Planning Centre like the Ganga, lays several conditions for the infatuated Raman, the painter of signs, to marry her and finally disappears. The parallel at the surface level is closer, but the difference shows the degeneration of life in the modern world (as in *The Waste Land*) but is itself purposeful, and it enhances the irony. Though there is some similarity between Daisy's passion for social works and Ganga's altruism, the difference is more glaring, and the very juxtaposition of the family-planning girl with the divine Ganga is comic. There is something anti - life about Daisy, and though Narayan makes his point (and probably because of it), the artistic value of the novel is rather questionable.

In *A Tiger for Malgudi* we find once again the full creative interplay of the fabulist imagination and the ironic mode. Here we have an inverted modern fable on a venerable tiger (who is the narrator also). The parallel between the animal and the human world is brought out with irony and sympathy and finally, as in *Animal Farm,* we do not know how to distinguish the two. If in the first part the parallel is between the tiger's fierceness and man's cruelty, the second part shows its affinity with the hermit: both attain a kind of freedom because they consider space and time as apparitions, and both are seeking their true identity. In one sense, the tiger is the Guru — because it always seeks freedom and has no sense of time or reckoning. When it is put in the cage, being used to the vastness and freedom of jungle life, it finds this an impossible condition of life :

> This was hell, as defined by my Master, an endless state of torment with no promise of relief or escape; I still had no conception that food could come one's way without a chase. These were the stages of knowing attained through suffering. I can hardly describe that kind of suffering, an emptiness, a helplessness, and a hopelessness behind the bars (9).

It also laughs at the master who thought he was the lord of the universe. Later, the tiger finds a kindred soul in the hermit who also obliterates his past and assumes a new name every time. He uses his powers to save the tiger and transform it inwardly, "working on the basis that, deep within, the core of personality is the same in spite of differing appearances and categories"(9). Ironically, the tiger is again put in a cage by the Master himself; but the last words of the Master (which are the last words of the novel also) are significant: "Both of us will shed our forms soon, and perhaps we could meet again. Who knows? So goodbye for the present." The fable establishes an ironic parallel between man and the tiger, and though it has no explicit link with any myth, it embodies the mythical notions of the self and becomes a myth of the self.

Structurally, too, all the novels from *Mr. Sampath* on have a mythic simplicity and a cyclic pattern. Most of them end where they began, and their various phases are linked with organic phases of life in the human and the natural world. Despite their bustle, ultimately they point to and emanate from a stillness in action.

In the time-scheme of the novels we also, see the counter-pointing of the mythical and ironic or human.

In *The Financial Expert* we see a sudden transportation of the everyday reality into a timeless order:

> Throughout the centuries, Srinivas felt this group was always three. Ram with his madness, his well-wishers with their panaceas and their apparatus of cure. Half the madness was his own doing, his lack of self-knowledge...sooner or later he shook off his madness

and realised his true identity though not in one birth, at least in a series of them.... The whole of eternity stretched ahead of one, there was plenty of time to shake off all follies. (208-09)

In *The Guide* also, the effect of timelessness in time is created by the clever juxtaposition of the past and the present. In *The Man-Eater of Malgudi* the cyclical pattern is imposed when, at the end, we are told, "he narrated again for my benefit the story of Bhasmasura, the unconquerable." But immediately against this recurrence of mythical time we have a specific time of history too: "When you are gone for lunch, it will be drying and ready." In one sense, here the human time imitates the cyclical pattern of myth. In *The Vendor of Sweets,* as well as in *A Tiger for Malgudi,* the concept of several *janmas* experienced in the present is mentioned. All these confirm our initial hypothesis that there is a perfect blending of the mythical and the ironic in the art and vision of R.K. Narayan. Mulk Raj Anand says that "in the newly emergent agro-industrial civilisations of Asia and Africa, the men and women of sensibility have entered the age of criticism, which seeks to relate the old myths to the new myths to synthesise the inner spaces to the outer spaces" (110), and then he adds that this is manifested even when modern writers like Raja Rao show "how the old wives' tale, though couched as a recital, absorbs the novel form by subtly interpenetrating the narrative with character analysis" (119). And this is relevant to R.K. Narayan, in whose novels the mythic or metaphoric vision is successfully penetrated by the metonymic or ironic mode; and in their vision and structure we can see the intersection of the timeless with time, the still point with the turning world still moving, of which the dance of Nataraja, which is also his favourite image, is the archetype.

Works Cited

Amur, G.S. "The River, the Lotus Pond, and the Ruined Temple: An Essay on Symbolism in R.K. Narayan's Novels." *Indian Readings in Commonwealth Literature*, Ed. G.S. Amur, et al. New Delhi : Sterling, 1985. 90-97.

Anand, Mulk Raj. "Old Myth-New Myth Recital Versus Novel." *Indian Literature of the Past Fifty Years*. Ed. C.D. Narasimhaiah. Mysore : Wesley, 1975. 110-15.

Berry, Margaret. "Ramayana and Narayana." *R.K. Narayan: A Critical Spectrum.* Ed. Bhagwat Goyal. Meerut: Shakskh, 1984. 58-66.

—, "R.K. Narayan: Lila and Literature." *Journal of Indian Writing in English*
     4.1 (July 1976): 1-3.

Naik, R.K. *The Ironic Vision*. New Delhi: Sterling, 1983.

Narayan, R.K. *The Financial Expert*. Mysore: Indian Thought, 1970.

—, *The Guide*. Mysore: London: Bodley, 1967.

—, *Mr Sampath*. Mysore: Indian Thought, 1973.

—, *A Tiger for Malgudi*. Mysore. Indian Thought, 1987.

Shepherd, Ron. "The Sublime and the Ridiculous: Allegory and Irony in R.K.
     Narayan's Fiction." *R.K. Narayan: A Critical Spectrum*. Ed. Bhagwat
     Goyal. Meerut: Shalakh, 1983. 90-88.

Walsh, William. *R.K Narayan: A Critical Appreciation*. London: Heinemann,
     1982.

4

ROMANTIC IRONY IN R. K. NARAYAN'S
THE PAINTER OF SIGNS

J.M.Q. DAVIES
(Northern Territory University)

The term "Romantic irony" has a paradoxical quality which, aside from its more specialised implications (which I shall consider subsequently), seems neatly to sum up two facets, or impulses, behind Narayan's art. For as astute and witty chronicles of Indian social mores, his novels form Western intertextual links with E.M. Forster, Jane Austen, Lawrence Sterne, and eighteenth-century satire. Yet his protagonists are typically individualists who often fall romantically in love or who tire and withdraw from the "fever and the fret" of modern Indian life in search of God or inner peace.

These two impulses, the Romantic and the ironic, are complexly blended in *The Painter of Signs,* a bitter-sweet romantic comedy that contains some of Narayan's most memorable comic characters and hilarious moments yet which darkens in tone as it progresses. Raman — whose credentials as calligrapher, lover of old books, and coffee-house philosopher make him something of an artist hero — is at once an "incurable Romantic," as the unsentimental Daisy says to him, and an amused, detached observer of her campaign to control the exploding population in the villages. As scenes unfold in which dramatic tension is cleverly sustained, Raman is always on stage; and events are largely presented from his point of view, which ultimately we come to endorse. Yet he is also consistently ironised by being portrayed as something of a comic Hercules at the Crossroads between Virtue and

Pleasure — a Renaissance pictorial formula that attained renewed intellectual currency in the eighteenth century through Lord Shaftesbury's discussion of it in his *Characteristics of Men, Manners, Opinions, Times* (1723-24). Thus Raman is amusingly presented as torn between reason and desire, between the attractions of bachelorhood and the attractions of Daisy; and later, having succumbed, between Daisy and his aunt, the forces of tradition and the need for change, the right to individual happiness and the claims of the collective. And his plight is further ironised by intermittent reminders that even the heroes of the *Ramayana* were not immune from the pangs of love, and that, in the words of the eccentric Town Hall Professor, in the end, "all this will pass."

The term "Romantic irony," in its technical sense, is more familiar to German than to English scholars and does not form part of the terminology of current literary theory. But there seems a certain *prima facie* appropriateness to one's invoking it in an eassay on Narayan in that Friedrich Schlegel, its chief theoretical exponent, was deeply interested in Indian culture, and like many of his Romantic contemporaries, he looked to the East for the renewal of literature.[1] "If only the treasures of the Orient were as accessible as those of Antiquity," he declared in his early *Dialogue on Poetry* (1799-1800), "what new sources of poetry could then flow from India.... It is in the Orient [that] we must look for the most sublime form of the Romantic" (87). What, however, makes Schlegel's theoretical insights in the *Dialogue* and the aphorisms from the *Lyceum* (1797) and *Athenaeum* (1798) of continuing relevance is that, with the intuitive intelligence that Coleridge, too, was gifted with, he put his finger on some of the artistic problems that have since emerged as characteristically modern. He perceived, for instance, that the modern writer "lacks a focal point, such as mythology was for the ancients" (81), a problem that Narayan addresses through his typological allusions to the *Ramayana* and *Mahabharata*. And like both Blake and Yeats, he regarded it as the function of poetry "to cancel the progression and laws of rationally thinking reason, and to transplant us once again into the beautiful confusion of imagination, into the original chaos of human nature, for which I know as yet no more beautiful symbol than the motley throng of the ancient gods" (86) — a sentiment with which, applied to the Indian pantheon, Narayan would surely be in sympathy. Schlegel also provides a precedent for the latitudinarian deployment of his terms, since "Romantic," for him, is not a period concept but an organic energising principle overriding the classical genres, now "ridiculous in their rigorous purity" (127), which he also found in Dante, medieval romance and Shakespeare. "Romantic poetry," he declared in a famous phrase, "is a progressive universal poetry" (140), and the "ultimate goal of all literature" is a harmonious synthesis of "the classical with the romantic" (112) — a goal he found most fully exemplified in Goethe, but which is also suggestive in the context of the fusion of Romantic and ironic elements in Narayan.

Romantic irony, which Schlegel sometimes confusingly calls Socratic irony and distinguishes as infinitely superior to rhetorical irony, is not comprehensively defined in his aphoristic writings, and what he meant by it has to be deduced from his various partial definitions. What, in essence, he was trying to do was to characterise the self-consciousness of the modern writer, and his awareness of the complexity and relativity of things in a skeptical demythologised post-Kantian world where God (if not yet dead) is disconcertingly unprovable. The immediate philosophical influence, in fact, was Johann Gotlieb Fichte, who between 1797 and 1800 was (with Friedrich Schleiermacher, Ludwig Tieck, and Dorothea Veit) a member of Schlegel's intimate circle of associates in Berlin. By going a step beyond Berkeley and affirming the ego as the ultimate reality, Fichte created, as Schlegel saw it, a solipsistic prison for the poet, alienating him from his subject matter and forcing him to acknowledge the relativity of truth. But by adopting an attitude at once of Romantic enthusiasm and ironic detachment towards his creation, an attitude in which "everything must be jest and yet seriousness, artless openness and yet deep dissimulation," the poet is able to escape the potential paralysis of this philosophical position and find a vehicle appropriate to expressing what Schlegel terms "a feeling of the insoluble conflict of the absolute and the relative, of the impossibility and necessity of total communication" (131).

The importance Schlegel attached to the poet's being gifted with the "divine breath of irony" and adopting this relexive "self-mirroring" or double point of view, explains his association of Socratic dialogue, which is inherently multiperspectival, with Romantic irony and why he regarded novels as "the Socratic dialogues of our time". It also explains why he held *Hamlet, Don Quixote,* and Goethe's *Wilhelm Meister* in such high esteem. That Romantic irony for Schlegel included a sense of the poignancy and pathos of man's existential plight bereft of absolute sanctions—of what we might perhaps term cosmic irony—may be inferred from the fact that he distinguishes it from verbal irony by comparing it to "ancient high tragedy," and consistently associates it with philosophy. Schlegel's poet, as Romantic ironist, thus has more in common with Schiller's self-conscious "sentimental" than his "naive" spontaneous poet, but he approaches his task with the philosophic playfulness that Schiller advocates in his *On the Aesthetic Education of Man in a Series of Letters* (1794).

Narayan is a master of irony in many of its modes, as has long been recognised.[2] He is essentially a mimetic novelist, of course, and though capable of Shandyan levity, does not indulge in Sterne's more radical defamiliarisation effects, which Tieck, Jean Paul, and Hoffmann adapted in experimenting with Romantic irony. Where Jean Paul, for instance, will puncture the illusion by thrusting himself and his problems as novelist directly upon the reader, Narayan's diffident sensitive personae, though often partial self-projections, are integrated into the dramatic action. The writer's world of publishers, printers, producers, and media entrepreneurs is amply represented in Narayan's fiction, but we do not encounter pages of Dr. Pal's pornography bound by mistake with the copy of *The Financial Expert* that we are reading, as we find excerpts from the biography of orchestra conductor Johannes Kreisler interrupting the text of Hoffmann's *Tomcat Murr* (1820) — jests which, as Oscar Walzel rightly says today, "Seem stale and ineffective" (234). And though Narayan's work includes interesting experiments with point of view (for instance, in *The Guide* and more recently in *A Tiger for Malgudi*, narrated by an Indian tomcat, "Raja the magnificent"), there is nothing as structurally multiperspectival as, say, Virginia Woolf's *The Waves* or Lawrence Durrell's *Alexandria Quartet*.

Yet through his use of a range of ironic strategies he typically achieves a richly refractive texture, inducing precisely the kind of "thoughtful "poetic reflection" that "multiplies" as in an endless series of mirrors," that Schlegel commends as putting "poetry in touch with philosophy" again (140-41). Both Narayan's and the Romantics' use of irony is more "philosophical" (in Schlegel's terms) than that of most eighteenth-century satire, because it is non-prescriptive: the post-Romantic writer does not ironise from the standpoint of firmly held ethical and social norms but induces us to ponder the complexity of things.

The Painter of Signs, though not without its detractors or its faults, deploys the full range of ironic techniques — verbal, situational, Sophoclean, double, symbolic, and (embracing all of these) Romantic — with consummate craftsmanship to create an enchanting novel that grows more sombre as the ironic resonances accrue, and which (like Jane Austen's) improves on second reading.[3] Most of the verbal (and some of the situational) irony is as immediately accessible as an oral performance of the *Ramayana* and accounts for the Shandyan lightness that is our first impression. In one of her rambling reminiscences, Raman's aunt, for instance, tells him how her

> "father was a priest and officiated at birthdays, funerals, and all kinds of religious functions and brought home his fee in the form of rice and vegetables and coconut and sugarcane. Occasionally he also brought home a cow, which, as you know, when gifted to a brahmin helps a dead man's soul to ford a difficult river in the next world."
>
> "How?" questioned the rationalist. (19)

Or when the village chiefman defies the intrepid Daisy by saying

> "There is an old shrine in a cave over there where barren women can go and pray and bear children. How would you explain it?" Daisy simply answered, "You should ask the priest of that temple," and Raman admired the courage and subtlety of her reply. (56)

Many of Raman's ironic comments as detached observer are internal, "communicating on two planes" (11) in a way that contributes to the dialogic effect that Schlegel recommended.[4] Complaining of grit on his freshly painted sign, the lawyer in an early scene protests, "'Do you want me to start my careeer with dirt on my name?' You are bound to have it sooner or later, why not now?" thinks Raman to himself, though aloud he replies more courteously. But Raman's own point of view is in turn placed in perspective through the deft use of what D. C. Muecke terms "irony of self-betrayal" (12).

> Must not make a fool of myself, he thought, a fellow whose outlook is to place sex in its place. To pursue a female after seeing only the upper half, above the desk — she might be one-legged, after all. But this is not sex which is driving me, but a normal curiosity about another person, that's all. (29)

In his subsequent progress as comic courtly lover, he repeatedly falls prey to self-delusion.

Situational irony of various kinds and degrees of seriousness is used to give dramatic tension to scenes which, told with less art, would

be indifferent. There is, for instance, a touch of Sophoclean irony of
fate about the way Raman is confronted by the very thing he seeks to
avoid: "He had absolutely avoided any thought of [Daisy].... But here
she was under his very roof" (45), listening to his reminiscing aunt.
Later, in the village, his "sense of irony [is] touched" by a situation in
which Daisy finds herself confronted by a priest equally fanatically
dedicated to the goddess of plenty: "This was going to prove the
antithesis of all her mission, defeat her entire business in life" (58).
The village sequence also illustrates the use of the multiple perspectives
that Schlegel thought essential to Romantic irony. First, we see Daisy
in the ascendant, lecturing on contraception, with the villagers gathered
round her "as if they were going to hear a *Ramayana* discourse" (56)—
an analogy that enriches by ironically contrasting old and new, sacred
and profane. And Raman, who has earlier made her blush red by
asking if she is a communist, is led by her fanaticism to ironic reflections
that have politically sobering implications: "Thank God, she is only
concerned with births and not death. Otherwise she'd be pestering
Yama to take away more people each day" (57). But almost immediately
there is a comic reversal when the tables are turned on the disconcerted
Daisy by the priest, who discloses knowledge of her past and proceeds
to harangue her about not tampering with God's designs. Further points
of view are expressed or represented by the villagers.

Situational irony is seen at its most farcical when the cart, driven
by a peasant who mistakes Raman and Daisy for newly-weds, breaks
down at night on the road home, and Raman advances "like Rudolph
Valentino in *The Sheik*" (74), only to discover next morning that he
has driven Daisy up a tamarind tree. And here again an ironising
perspective on their quarrel is provided by the innocently knowing
carter, who refuses to rise from his knees until the lovers get back into
the cart: for though ignorant of their relationship, he sees their tiff as
in the eternal scheme of things. Raman's reactions, by contrast, are
extreme, and on his return we see him in the classic dilemmic situation
of what Muecke terms "double irony" — fearful lest he be accused of
rape yet grieving at the loss of Daisy. Generally, the minor characters
(representing the normal flow of daily life in India) tend to ironise the
main protagonists and prevent their actions seeming stagey; and the
poignant "little ironies" (in Hardy's phrase) of their existence — the
village peasant who mistakes Daisy for a doctor able to abort his wife
or the accountant who treats the office as a refuge from his garrulous
spouse — deepen the pathos of the novel.

But it is only with the tragi-comic reversal and situational ironies of the finale, where Raman finds that he has lost his beloved aunt but not gained a wife to replace her, that the advantages of Schlegel's comprehensive notion of Romantic irony over more technical modes becomes apparent. The dialogical debate between progress and tradition in the village is recapitulated in the contrast between Daisy and Raman's aunt, who in their simplicity and dedication — the one to contraception the other to her nephew and her faith — turn out to have more in common than we had suspected. Raman himself is no longer, as in the village, the detached observed but in the dilemmic situation of a Hercules forced to choose between them. One of the more poignantly amusing closing sequences, which uses the comic technique of incremental repetition with delightful freshness, is that in which Raman reflects on his aunt's final instructions:

> "Remember the rice in the bag is cleaned.... You won't have to buy gingelly oil for at least six months.... You must be careful to see that insects don't get into it, and you must tell whoever is going to look after these things." This was her manner of referring to Daisy, always indirectly and wanting to forget her if possible. "And then take care to air the pickles ...." Raman was getting an inkling of the enormous industry at home that had gone on unseen in minute detail, to keep him properly nourished day after day for thirty years. "The milkman comes with the cow at four thirty in the morning." How would Daisy fit into this scheme? Would she stand beside a cow at dawn, or keep the oil jar aired regularly? Unthinkable. (128-29)

What this passage induces us and incipiently Raman, to reflect on is both the value and the futility of the traditional way, the justice but also the losses entailed in Daisy's rejection of it all. And this is precisely the reflective mode of Schlegel's notion of Romantic irony, conceived not merely as prismatic complexity of point of view but as a philosophical awareness of the existential ironies and ambiguity of life. The aunt's little acts may be meaningless, but they are done with love; and her faith in the good offices of a gifted cow in the next world may be an illusion, but it has given her direction in life and the courage to face change and death with equanimity. Daisy's rejection of everything she stands for, her preference for a "Gandharva-style marriage, as easily snapped as made" (132), and her dedication to her work for the community are all understandable and arguably progressive, but they entail impoverishment and loss, as her indifference to Raman's cultural interests and her slightly masculine voice imply.

We may guess where Narayan ultimately stands in all of this, but his discreet narrative voice is never one-sidedly prescriptive. For, as the Master tells Raja the Magnificent in *A Tiger for Malgudi*, "Human ties cannot be defined in just black-and-white terms" (60); and it is masters of Romantic irony such as Narayan who make us fully aware of their complexity.

Notes

1.   Friedrich Schlegel's major work on India was *On the Language and Wisdom of India* (1811). His less brilliant elder brother, August Wilhelm, held the chair of Oriental Languages at the University of Bonn from 1817 and devoted the rest of his life to Sanskrit and Indian studies. The high esteem in which Schlegel's early theoretical writings have been held in Germany can be gauged from E.R. Curtius's remark in his *European Literature and the Latin Middle Ages*, trans. W. Trask (Princeton: Princeton UP, 1952), that "in Germany we have Friedrich Schlegel... and beginnings" (16).

2.   See, for example, H. Williams, *Indo-Anglian Literature, 1800-1970: A Survey* (Bombay: Orient Longman, 1977) 54-63; S.P. Bhardwaj, *"The Painter of Signs:* An Analysis." *Perspectives on R.K. Narayan.* Ed. Arman Ram. (Atlantic Highlands, NJ: Humanities, 1982) 173; and Jayant K. Biswal, *A Critical Study of the Novels of R.K. Narayan* (New Delhi: Nirmal, 1987) 77-110.

3.   See C.N. Srinath, "R.K. Narayan's Comic Vision: Possibilities and Limitations." *World Literature Today* 55 (1977): 419. The main weakness of the novel seems to me to be a Shavian tendency in the main characters to the ever-explicit discussion of ideas.

4.   See William Walsh, *R.K. Narayan: A Critical Appreciation* (Chicago: U of Chicago P, 1982) 156. In his emphasis on the dialogic aspect of Romantic irony, Schlegel anticipates Mikhail Bakhtin, for whom, however, dialogy is not necessarily ironic. See M.M. Bakhtin, *The Dialogic Imagination*, trans. M. Holquist (Austin: U of Texas P, 1981).

5.   Biswal (n.2) maintains that "there is no definite ironic pattern in which the characters gradually mature into realisation and knowledge" (107). But it seems to me that Raman is a distinctly more aware person by the end of the novel, and even Daisy comes to recognise in a more than merely theoretical way that marriage is less important than her work.

6. See David Scott Philip, *Perceiving India* (New York: Envoy, 1986), who writes that "there is, Narayan seems to say, something inhumanly defeminising about women's liberation" (121).

Works Cited

Muecke, D.C. *The Compass of Irony.* London: Methuen , 1969.

Narayan, R.K. *The Painter of Signs.* London: Heinemann, 1977.

Schlegel, Friedrich. *Dialogue on Poetry and Literary Aphorisms.* Trans. and ed. Ernst Behler and Roman Struc. University Park: Pennsylvania State UP, 1968.

Walzel, Oscar, *German Romanticism.* Trans. A.E. Lussky. New York: Capricorn, 1963.

5

HISTORY, MAYA, DHARMA : THE NOVELS OF R.K. NARAYAN

MICHAEL GORRA
(Smith College)

My subject is a dual one : first, the ways in which the novel, that most Western and historically conditioned of genres, has in the work of R.K. Narayan been adapted to Indian — or rather, Hindu — conceptions of character, history, and even the physical world itself; and second, the ways in which a Western reader responds to that adaptation. You will, I hope, forgive me if my treatment of that second subject is largely implicit in the terms of my argument. It has been a great deal on my mind, but I've not yet been able to say much about it directly. I should say, too, that my argument takes the form of a commentary on the narrative structure of what I take to be Narayan's finest two novels, *The Guide* and *The Financial Expert,* and that this will involve reminding you of some of the details of their plots.

Let me start not with Narayan himself but with a moment in Ruth Prawer Jhabvala's *The Householder.* You'll remember that when his wife Indu goes for a few weeks' visit to her parents, Jhabvala's protagonist, Prem, realises that without her he doesn't feel as if he is "a family man with duties and responsibilities." He's no longer a student, but in her absence he is not quite a householder either. It's as if he's stranded between two stages of life, two separate *ashramas;* and without the shelter those stages offer, Prem feels as if "he belonged nowhere, was nothing, was nobody" — as if there is no Prem apart from the worldly circumstances that define his *dharma* (his duty), his role in life and the behaviour that role requires.

Here I will turn to Narayan himself, for his work depends, as the titles of his books suggest, on exploring just that question of the relation between the self and its social role : *The Bachelor of Arts, The English Teacher, The Vendor of Sweets, The Painter of Signs.* Nearly all his fiction takes place in the small South Indian town of Malgudi. It is a sleepy place, so peaceful that in the novels set before Independence the British presence seems limited to a few statues and the Albert Mission College; it is almost entirely Hindu, and so unmarked by communal strife. One can date the action of most novels within a few years — not only Ruth Prawer Jhabvala's, but also Raja Rao's *Kanthapura* or those of Anita Desai or Mulk Raj Anand — but Narayan's seem abstracted from history. Or no — not abstracted so much as marked by a sense of history's irrelevance to Malgudi life. Rosie, in *The Guide,* comes from a family of *devadasis,* temple dancers, who " are viewed as public women." But she now dances professionally, as a almost respectable exponent of traditional culture. Yet while that move from the shrine to the secular stage is typical of classical Indian dance at mid-century, Narayan makes no attempt to see her as a representative figure, as what George Lukacs called a typical character of her age—as indeed Jhabvala does with Prem or the main character of her first novel, *Amrita.* Or perhaps he does. For through her disastrous effect on the title figure, Raju, Rosie suggests the disruptive power of all change, including the historical one that has made her career possible. But she soon leaves Malgudi behind, allowing its inhabitants to resume the habitual and ahistorical rhythm of their lives.

V.S. Naipaul has written that Narayan is "inimitable." He is inimitable because his indifference to historical flux, his tendency to treat all change as maya (illusion) paradoxically depends on his own precise location within that flux. Narayan was born in 1907 into an orthodox brahmin family, and in the princely state of Mysore; born, that is, at almost the last moment and in the last place where one could maintain an image of an India that did not seem to change. The outer world of Partition, Five-Year Plans, war, sectarian violence — none of it seems to touch Malgudi. Neither do the natural disasters of flood, famine or disease. In consequence, Anita Desai writes, many of Narayan's Indian readers feel that he doesn't capture "the chaos, the drift, the angst that characterises a society in transition and that his 'rootedness' is a relic

of another, a pastoral era now shaken and threatened beyond recovery."
And his stance is impossible for younger writers, at work in the India
that Desai herself reveals in *In Custody,* a world of nylon saris and
Japanese electronics. What Narayan offers instead, Desai suggests, is
an evocation of "the India that is capable of absorbing change and of
transforming it into the perpetual." Yet that evocation, like all pastoral,
is in itself a response to change; and the bulk of his readers find
Narayan's "rootedness" reassuring, even as they deny its relevance to
their own lives.

The Guide opens with Raju, newly released from prison, taking
shelter in the ruins of an ancient shrine along the river bank. He has
had some education, and it is moreover "in his nature to get involved
in other people's interests and activities" (6). So when the villager
Velan mistakes him for a swami, Raju is able to find the words the role
demands. Nevertheless, it makes him feel "like an actor who was
always expected to utter the right sentence" (11), and so he eventually
tells Velan his life's story, trying to prove that he is "not a saint." No
saint indeed. Raju has spent much of his earlier career as that most
engaging of charlatans, a tour guide of the sort who doesn't even know
whether the places her recommends are worth visiting. One day Rosie
and her archaeologist husband Marco come to him. Raju shows Marco
the cave paintings he wants to see, but he also involves himself in
Rosie's activities. He encourages her in the dancing that Marco has
demanded that she give up; and when she leaves Marco for him, Raju
becomes that impresario behind her enormously successful string of
public recitals. "I was puffed up with the thought of how I had made
her...," he says, "there was no limit to my self-congratulation" (161).
And no limit to his spending, either, until one day he forges Rosie's
signature on a receipt for some jewellery and goes to jail because of it.

All this he tells Velan one year when the rains are so late that the
harvest looks as if it might fail. A mix-up has made the villagers
believe that their swami has promised to fast until it rains, they believe
that their swami has promised to fast until it rains, they believe, in fact,
that his fasting will bring the rain. Raju has said has nothing of the
kind, but feels trapped by the role he has so successfully played. he
believes that "the time had come for him to be serious — to attach
value to his own words," to make the inner life of the rogue match
the swami's public role. He tries one last time to break free, by telling
Velan his story, but when at its conclusion the villager still calls him

"Swami," Raju feels he must continue the fast, even though he doesn't believe it will do any good. On the twelfth day he is helped down to the river to pray :

> He stepped into it, shut his eyes and turned toward the mountain, his lips muttering the prayer. Velan and another held him each by an arm. The morning sun was out by now; a great shaft of light illuminated the surroundings. It was difficult to hold Raju on his feet, as he had a tendency to flop down. They held him as if he were a baby. Raju opened his eyes, looked about, and said, "Velan, it's raining in the hills, I can feel it coming up under my feet, up my legs—" He sagged down. (220).

And the novel ends. But what happens? Is it really raining in the hills, or is Raju simply so weakened by hunger, so near death, that he mistakes the water around his legs for rain? If it is raining, how does he know? And did his fast cause it? And does he even believe what he says, or is he simply giving his audience what they want, one last and probably fatal time? Narayan leaves those questions open, and perhaps one's view of the ending of *The Guide* depends on where one stands in terms of things like swamis, and miracle, and prayer. The orthodox may read the novel as what Naipaul calls a "Hindu fable," but that needn't prevent the strictly secular from taking it as a comedy in which Raju is caught, if movingly so, by his habit of avoiding "the direct and bald truth." And for those in between, for those of us who aren't Hindu but who do recognise what Naipaul himself describes as the "basic human hunger of the unseen," the very openness of the novel's ending offers a way in which that hunger may, however, briefly, be assuaged.

Yet a strictly secular — or a strictly Western — reading of *The Guide* seems finally incomplete, though to say this is not to claim anything about Narayan's personal orthodoxy. But is to emphasise the degree to which he has been shaped by traditional Hindu thought and by Hindu conceptions of human character, above all. Just before Raju's collapse, a journalist asks him if he has always been a yogi. "Yes," he replies, " more or less." One laughs — Raju the dishonest tour guide has seemed so very un-yogi-like. But suppose one takes his words seriously? Before he was less of a yogi; now he is more. Always he has been a guide of one kind or another, someone showing people how to get what they want they want, whether as a tour guide, as an impresario of traditional culture, or now as a spiritual guide, a swami. The whole

action of the novel has, in fact, been a process of discovering just what
sort of guide he is, of becoming more the yogi that he has always been.

Character in Narayan is fixed in a way that in Western literature
is more common on the stage than in a novel. For as his titles suggest,
dharma in Narayan's work functions very much like a Hindu equivalent
of the *caracteres* of seventeenth-century French comedy. As Moliere
has his embodiments of vices, his miser and his misanthrope, so Narayan
has his financial expert and his sweet-vendor, figures who can no more
escape their *dharma* than Tartuffe can escape the consequences of his
own hypocrisy. But where the vices of Moliere's characters as so innate
that never thinks to explain their origin, Narayan's characters find that
their natures have been determined by the force of external events, over
which they have at best the illusion of control. Raju takes no active role
in shaping his own career : he becomes a tour guide by accident,
because other people expect it of him; so, too, he becomes a swami. His
only actions are negative ones and grow from his dual lusts for Rosie
and for money. Then he is seized by an egotism that makes him into
a type of the demonic man described in the *Bhagavad Gita* : "Self-
aggrandizing, stubborn, /drunk with wealth and pride." But on the
river bank that egotism falls away, and in the end *The Guide* shows
how Raju comes to fulfil his role — how he makes his inner life match
his fixed and determined outer circumstances, performing the *dharma*
from which the *maya* of his affair with Rosie, his attachment to the
illusory things of this world, had distracted him.

Yet the longer the Western reader looks at Narayan's novels, the
stranger they become. For *The Guide* also suggests that the things that
happen to Raju, the events that determine this situation (and through
that his character), may not be entirely extrinsic to him. "It is written
on the brow of some," he tells Velan, "that they shall not be left alone.
I am one such, I think." But which comes first : What's written on his
brow, or the fact that people won't leave him alone ? On the one hand,
his character, his *dharma,* is innate; on the other, it seems determined
by external circumstances. Yet perhaps there's no final difference between
them, not in a philosophy that denies the Western divorce of subjective
experience from the objective world. Both are instead aspects of Brahman,
the spiritual essence that underline all things. When he goes bankrupt
at the end of *The Financial Expert,* Narayan's protagonist Margayya
feels that "he had lost all right to personal life." Yet his surrender of
his earlier and illusory belief that "man...could make his own present

and future" allows him to find a peace he hadn't known in the days
of his greed and financial success; to become a man who is, as the *Gita*
says, "at one with the infinite spirit, /serene in himself," and who
therefore "does not grieve or crave." Once Margayya accepts that the
self can't control its circumstances, that self paradoxically becomes
inviolable : simultaneously determined by and yet separate from those
circumstances; in the world but not bound by it. And that does indeed
begin to make the Western separation of the soul from the world seem
as if it is indeed the creation of *maya,* a purely arbitrary distinction.

The *Financial Expert* stands with *The Guide* as the richest of
Narayan's novels. When the books opens, Margayya has for years been
spending his days under a banyan tree outside a bank in Malgudi, as
if he were himself a part of India's unchanging landscape. And he, too,
is a guide of sorts, for his name means "one who showed the way." He
shows "the way out," that is, "to those in financial trouble," helping
peasants fill in the bank's forms, advancing them small sums, earning
for his services an anna here, a rupee there. The name has been given
him by his clients, and it defines him so completely that he has almost
forgotten that his given name is Krishna. One day the bank's secretary
tells Margayya to move along. And in response to this enforced change
in the given circumstances of his life, Margayya swears to make so
much money that one day "'The secretary will have to call me 'Mister'
and stand up when I enter.'" A priest tells him to perform a forty-day
puja to Lakshmi, goddess of wealth, and it is while getting the red lotus
he needs for the ritual that he meets Dr. Pal, one of the energetic
charlatans so common in Narayan's fiction. Dr. Pal has written a book
in which he claims to have fused Havelock Ellis and the *Kama-Sutra,*
into *Bed-Life, or the Science of Marital Happiness,* pornography
masquerading as a marriage-manual. And after completing his *puja*
Margayya meets Dr. Pal again, and receives the manuscript of *Bed-Life*
as a gift. Its publication makes his fortune.

The rest of the novel details the roller-coaster of Margayya's finances.
He gets a motor-car, opens a bank of his own and finally bribes an
astrologer to fiddle with his son's horoscope so that he can make a
good match for the boy. For at the height of his success he comes to
believe that

These were not days when he had to wait anxiously on a verdict
of the stars : he could afford to ask for his own set of conditions

and get them. He no longer believed that man was a victim of
circumstances or fate — but that man was a creature who could
make his own present and future, provided he worked hard and
remained watchful (185).

How far away Margayya seems here from the character who had let his
customers choose his name, or from the Raju who believed his fate was
written on his brow. Yet, in trying to control his own fate, Margayya
has begun to act like a character in a Western novel; and one knows,
therefore, that his comeuppance cannot be far away, that he must be
pulled back toward an acceptance of his *dharma*. For Margayya's greed
makes him, as Narayan writes, "like one possessed," one of the demonic
men the *Gita* describes as hoarding "wealth in stealthy ways to satisfy
their desires." And eventually he grows so excited by the sheer flow of
money that he offers his depositors the impossible interest rate of 10
per cent a month, simply to accumulate a pile of cash he doesn't need.
Inevitably he is deluged with customers, inevitably the rumour spreads
that their deposits are not safe. The run on his bank ruins him — and
yet his surrender to the "tide" of his angry creditors also leads him to
a sense of peace I have described above. And in the novel's last
paragraph Margayya says that he will soon go back to sitting under that
banyan tree, resuming the sort of life he had when the novel started.

One recognises a traditional comic pattern as well as a Hindu truth
in the circularity of the novel's structure. But that fusion of comedy and
religion depends on something more than the novel's circular structure.
The would-be Margayya prays to Lakshmi in a room

> filled with the scent of incense, camphor, sandal dust and jasmine.
> All this mingled perfume uplifted the heart and thoughts of
> Margayya. He was filled with a feeling of holiness — engendered
> by the feel of the red silk at his waist. He was gratified at the
> thought of his wife's obedience. "She is quite accommodating," he
> reflected (69-70).

Long shot for comedy, Chaplin said; close-up for tragedy. It is a rule
that Narayan observes throughout his work — above all in depicting
his character's interior lives. Margayya is filled with holiness as the
room is filled with incense, and Narayan's style makes no distinction
between them. He doesn't attempt, that is, to dramatise the experience
of holiness, but instead simply reports it as an objective fact, on the
same order as the way the room smells. The language throughout

remains plain, simple, unmarked by emotional shading of any kind. That style keeps Margayya at a distance, in a long shot that lets us laugh at him precisely because of our inability to enter his thoughts and dreams and fears. For Narayan's "whole achievement," as the critic Meenakshi Mukherjee writes, "depends on his capacity to remain un-involved" (170). She means that in political terms, comparing him to his contemporaries Raja Rao and Mulk Raj Anand, and suggesting that his evocation of an unchanging traditional life depends on keeping politics out. But that uninvolvement extends as well to the way his style holds his characters at arm's length, keeping the reader from feeling as if his emotions are bound up with their fates. One wants Prem and Indu in *The Householder* to have a good marriage, but Narayan's work leaves one fascinated by and yet indifferent to Margayya, indifferent even to Raju's collapse at the end of *The Guide*. And that indifference, while inseparable from Narayan's comedy, seems finally a cultivation of the *Gita* ideal of non-attachment, the stylistic equivalent of the relaxation Margayya feels when he renounces his rights to a personal life.

Narayan lacks her savagery, but in Western fiction the contemporary writer he most closely resembles is Muriel Spark. Both writers see their characters *sub specie aeternitatis,* concerned only with their souls and not their bodies. (Indeed, Spark does awful things to those bodies as a way of underlining their unimportance.) But it's not so easy for the reader; and both writers, crucially, are comic ones. Comedy offers a secular justification for an indifference that finally grows out of religious belief. For as Mukherjee writes, individual fulfilment "has always been alien to Indian tradition, especially when it is achieved at the cost of duty to family" (67). Margayya's experiment in individualism has indeed threatened that duty; he just barely manages to keep their very house from being claimed by his creditors. His realisation at the end of the novel, then that he has "lost all right to personal life," and the sense of peace that is inseparable from that loss — these are something more than comic. For Narayan's comedy is in the end but a way of suggesting that all change, all history, is *maya*. Yet one's essentially ahistorical *dharma* does not change and (because of that) shows the way to transcendence and peace. The conclusion of *The Financial Expert* amounts to an assertion of the power, the inescapability, and even the justness of tradition; it suggests not simply that his is the inevitable way of the world but that this is the way the world should be. India endures, Narayan seems to say, in making Margayya take up his

position beneath the banyan tree once more; it endures now as it was
and will be, even with motor cars and movie houses and novelists
writing in English. And it is that affirmation, perhaps, that makes his
work not only a reassuring point of stability in a rapidly changing
country but a bit unsettling as well.

That unsettling quality seems to me especially marked at the moment
early in the novel when Margayya is accosted by a beggar who points
at a "sheet-covered object." " 'An orphan's body,'" the beggar says,
"'help us to bury him.'" The moneylender shudders, surrenders a coin,
and begins to think:

> He knew what it meant. A group of people seized upon an unclaimed
> dead body, undertook to give it a burial and collected a lot of
> money for it. He knew that they celebrated it as a festive occasion...
> [they gave] a gorgeous funeral to the body...and were left with so
> much money at the end of it all that they drank and made merry
> for three or four days and gave up temporarily their normal jobs,
> such as scavenging, load-carrying, and stone-quarrying. It made
> Margayya reflective. (28)

Naipaul has written that "Narayan's novels did not prepare me for the
distress of India" — did not prepare him because they do not show the
starving, the dying, the diseased; offer no account of the dirt, and the
squalor, and the smell. That comment might seem mistaken when set
against the passage I've just quoted. Yet that passage is atypical, the
only account of India's "distress" in the novel, and one of the few such
in all Narayan's work. And it is not, crucially, an attempt to defamiliarise
the world that ordinarily passes unnoticed before one's eyes, not the
observation of a detached narrator so familiar to the Western reader
from Dickens or Zola. "He knew what it meant," Narayan writes; and
what follows are Margayya's thoughts about the way such beggars
work.

The sight leads Margayya into a meditation on the mystical power
of money, a meditation that confirms his desire to change the way he
lives. So while the passage tells us about Indian street life, it also serves
a dramatic purpose within the novel as a whole, in a way that ensures
that Narayan's Indian readers will not object to the scene as a bit of
degraded exotica for the Western market. (We Indians know what such
things look like already, the argument goes — why, then, do our
novels need to describe them?) As such, it seems a neat and economical

piece of work. But place it against Narayan's statement, in the postscript to his 1987 novel *Talkative Man*, that in reading, he "ruthlessly" skips over all "laboured detail and description of dress, deportment, facial features, furniture, food and drinks," and has no interest in rendering such details himself. His words suggest a lack of interest in the physical world, a sense of its irrelevance to the main business of the narrative. Those beggars, that corpse, have no independent existence within the fiction. They matter only in so far as they affect Margayya's thoughts.

Let me quote here from Naipaul's account of Narayan in *An Area of Darkness* (1964), for it contains a troubling and perhaps unanswerable charge. Narayan's "virtues," he writes :

> are Indian failings magically transmuted.... Some years ago he told me in London that, whatever happened, India would go on. He said it casually; it was a conviction so deep it required no stressing. It is a negative attitude, part of that older India which was incapable of self-assessment. It has this result: the India of Narayan's novels is not the India the visitor sees. He tells an Indian truth. Too much that is overwhelming has been left out, too much has been taken for granted. (227-28)

Usually one praises a writer for showing something other than what the visitor sees. But Narayan's "Indian truth" depends, Naipaul argues, on a "defect of vision" that allows the novelist to ignore what is plain to the most casual of tourists. It depends on taking the material world, if not precisely as *maya,* then so much for granted that one barely notices it. Of course, the details of India's "distress" are not the only story the country has to tell. Yet they are a part of the story, as are the other things Narayan omits: the colours of fruit and of clothing, the smells of the bazaar, the shape of a face, or the layout of a city square. The attitude behind such omissions has, perhaps, always provided a refuge from the difficulties of Indian life, a way of living as if those difficulties don't matter; as if, as the *Gita* says, "Weapons do not cut..../Fire does not burn...." Yet while that stance is a defence against distress, it is also, Naipaul writes, one of the "attitudes that contributed to the calamity." And so one hears in Narayan no note of criticism, finds no sense of all the ways in which a traditional order might prove a limiting one; no sense of all the things one might see about that order if only one could defamiliarise it enough to see it all.

Naipaul compares Narayan— and indeed the Indian novel as a whole — to its Japanese equivalent, which "also began as part of the mimicry of the West." But the Japanese, he writes, "are possessed of a way of looking .... a hunger for the seen," and their novels are "an expression of a concern with men"(229). I cannot speak of the Japanese novel. But think for a moment of Japanese visual arts, of the woodblock print. However distorted its spatial relations may see, one cannot doubt its fidelity to the details of the visible world: the specificity, the meticulous precision with which it depicts this courtesan, that view of Fuji. And compare those prints to the sketchily abstract landscapes and formulaic portraits one finds in Rajput paintings of Rama's or Krishna's mythic adventures. A way of looking. And one remembers that Naipaul has said as well that as a genre the novel is a "response to the here and now," to people caught in a precisely seen and rendered historical moment, a moment whose uniqueness is denied by Narayan's statement that whatever happens, India will go on, "Unlike the Greeks," Nehru has written, "and unlike the Chinese and the Arabs, Indians in the past were not historians." Instead, he adds, they relied on what "the imagined history of the Epics," in which myth is indistinguishable from fact" (56). It is an historical judgment of the sort Narayan himself never makes — and in reading *The Financial Expert* one begins to see a connection between the possession of an historical sense and an appreciation of the visible world. For Narayan deals with history only be denying its importance, in much the same way as the orthodox Hindu denies the existence of the physical world. Both are forms of *maya,* for both depend on a concern with material reality, and Narayan's omission of visual detail is finally inextricable from Malgudi's abstraction from history.

Works Cited

Mukherjee, Meenakshi. *The Twice-Born Fiction: Themes and Techniques of the Indian Novel in English.* New Delhi: Heinemann, 1971.

Naipaul, V.S. *An Area of Darkness.* New York: Macmillan, 1964.

Narayan, R.K. *The Financial Expert.* Chicago: U of Chicago P, 1981.

—, *The Guide.* New York: Viking, 1958.

Nehru, Jawaharlal. *The Discovery of India.* Oxford: Oxford UP, 1954.

6

R.K. NARAYAN AND PATRICK WHITE AS SHORT-STORY TELLERS

H.H. ANNIAH GOWDA
(University of Mysore)

E.M. Forster once said, in a sort of drooping, regretful voice, "Oh yes, oh dear yes, the novel tells a story." And in his Postscript to *Talkative Man*, R.K. Narayan writes,

> I had planned *Talkative Man* as a full-length novel .... While it progressed satisfactorily enough, it would not grow .... (it) is too long to be a short story, but is it too short for novel? I prefer the shorter form, because it gives me scope for elaboration of details, but within certain limits; I can take up a variety of subjects and get through each in a reasonable time, while a novel ties me down to a single theme for at least two years! When I am at work on a novel, I imagine that I am keeping a crowd of characters waiting outside my door. (120-21)

Yet Patrick White, the author of several epic novels, felt constrained by the limits of the short-story form; short stories, he claimed, he did not really very much like to write. But as he points out in *Flaws in the Glass: A Self-Portrait* and in some of the letters that are included in David Marr's biography of him, he also thought that short stories were a very useful means of breaking a writing block and of limbering up for an attack on a novel.

These statements illustrate the principal tasks of the writer of the short story: to tell a story on a small canvas and to decide what things have to be excluded. A short-story writers, White and Narayan demonstrate how the controlling ironies establish a balance between the surface of social trivia and the hidden psychological and spiritual truths. As V.S. Naipaul has phrased it, Narayan's stories illustrate "the Hindu response to the world"; however, it is considerably more difficult to summarise White's stories; he has problems in accommodating his expansive imagination to the limits of the short story. *The Burnt Ones* has a title that speaks for itself: the characters are mauled and are lonely; *The Cockatoos*, with its explanatory subtitle, *Shorter Novels and Stories*, broadly explored the modern destruction of love. White's novels, like Faulkner's, sometimes grow out of stories: *The Eye of the Storm* clearly had its beginning in "Dead Roses," the first story in *The Burnt Ones*. White, who was sexually ambivalent, claimed for himself special insights into intimate rigours of marriage that his characters undergo, the hunger of the heart for a human companionship that might assuage the loneliness that haunts them all. He emphasises loneliness, the contrast between the ugly and the beautiful side in a very Joycean story like "Down at the Dump." The narrative, which ironically juxtaposes a funeral and a cheerful day's outing to a rubbish dump, use the stream-of-consciousness technique to revive the spirit of the dead woman, Daise Morrow, a promiscuous woman. This technique is foreign to Narayan, who grew up in an orthodox middle-class brahmin family and contemplates small men and the joys and sorrows of his characters in his fictional world of Malgudi. Narayan seems to be quite at home in short stories of restricted social setting. In small proportions he sees just beauties.

Nara_ in and White, as short story writers, are as different as can be. White's themes are big and elaborate. "The Twitching Colonel," which appeared in *London Mercury* in April 1937, and "Cocotte," which *Horizon* printed in 1940, are concerned with big themes and big persons. "The Twitching Colonel," in mannered, modern prose, is about a fire incident that recurs in *The Aunt's Story*; it is about an old, alcoholic, Indian Army colonel's stream of consciousness playing over a distant past (curiously enough, of the exoticism of Hindu civilisation opposed to that of the Raj). The colonel is alone in the battered splendours of London's Pimlico; his only companion, a landlady, values him for his antecedents, his medals, and his stories of India. It is very much a Paul Scott story. The tragic story ends with a heavy finger pointing the moral note: "We creep away. It is something we do not understand We are afraid." This recalls the ending of *The English Teacher,* in which the protagonist has telepathic communication with his dead wife: "The boundaries of our personalities suddenly dissolved. It was a moment rare, immutable joy — a moment for which one feels grateful to life and death." Narayan is a happy novelist who contemplates the lesser life that goes on below; tentacles of deep philosophy do not disturb the concept of Malgudi. The reputation of Narayan as the creator of Malgudi and the oddities of his many small characters has grown with healthy slowness over his long career as a novelist. It has grown like young Swami who, through his school, cultivated playmates, played cricket matches against the Y.M.U; and bid goodbye to Rajam, Mani and Swaminathan at the Malgudi station, making his companions uniformly sad.

Swami and Friends, which contains delightful pen-portraits of young men who roam and romp about the streets of Malgudi, established the topographical sense of the place so natural to a writer true to his emotions. These characters are distinctly Indian. White, who worked in different continents, draws his characters from various countries: Greece, England, Australia. Narayan's canvas is small, but his characters are vivid. The tale-telling impulse is irrepressibly fecund and carries the main character through various episodes big and small — but all memorable.

White's stories in *The Cockatoos,* mostly set in Australia, emphasise loneliness, though not to the complete exclusion of poverty and sickness. The Makridies family of "The Full Belly," who survive on boiled dandelions in Athens (while occupied by the Germans in the Second World War), are nicely delineated. They can sell their talents or themselves for food. Royal Natwick, in "Five-Twenty," is confined to a wheelchair by a combination of hernia, heart, and "arthritis," but his wife assures him of good care. White's characters are wealthy enough but not healthy enough. Loneliness is another problem that White handles, and it is caused mostly by the evil of drink. His people attempt violent remedies to overcome their isolation; Clem Dowson, for example, in "A Woman's Hand," gives up his lifelong self-sufficiency to marry, late in life, a woman chosen for him by Evelyn Fazackerley. It is a domestic story that nears Narayan's craft in the discussion of how to make cumquat jam and of a woman's role at home. But the marriage of Clem and Nesta is a near-disaster. The atmosphere of "The Night of the Prowler" is as fierce as one would expect from someone for whom the full tide of life has just begun to run. The conventional, over-protected daughter of a heavy-handed middle-class

family, Felicity is released from her carefully schooled frustration by a
prowler who breaks into the house and tries to "rape" her. Unfortunately,
when she is about to yield, the prowler turns out to be as impotent as
Faulkner's Popeye, but without his resourcefulness. Felicity's supposed
violation enables her to discard the passionless diplomat to whom she
is engaged, and she embarks on a quest for real experience that will
"violate her aloneness." Failed by man, Felicity turns to God. Her
ultimate revelation — if that is what it is — is one of total Beckettian
nihilism: "I am nothing. I believe in nothing. And nothing's a noble
faith. Nobody can hurt nothing. So you've no reason for being afraid:
(166-67). What cold comfort for a young girl who urgently seeks
company!

In Narayan's *The English Teacher,* the husband who loses his wife
keeps himself alive by establishing a telepathic communication with his
dead wife. He feels the presence of his wife by his wide, and this
enables him to resume his normal work. It is like Tagore's Smarana
Geeta: his dead wife is included in *Gitanjali:*

> In desperate hope I go and search for her in all
> my rooms; I find her not ....
> Let me for once feel that lost sweet touch in the
> allness of the Universe. (L XXXVII)

The English Teacher has a special biographical relevance for the literary
critic. (Narayan complains that some find the latter part of the novel
sentimental.) Those who have given their devotion to the story must
look at it in the light of the spiritual experience the author underwent.
I might quote G.K. Chesterton's remark that when people cease to
believe in something, they will believe in anything. Faith plays a role
in one's life. Narayan's comment in *My Days* is interesting: "Out of
all this experience a view of personality or self or soul developed,
which has remained with me ever since" (182). This comes naturally
to one who has grown up on the *Gita*'s dictum "Easwara Sarva Bhootanam"
(God lives in all). White, who is foreign to this concept, destroys
Felicity of "The Night of the Prowler." White considered himself a
Christian and did not want to divorce Christianity from other religions:
"In my books I have lifted bits from various religions in trying to come
to a better understanding. Now, as the world becomes more pagan, one
has to lead people in the same direction in a different way." In *The
Solid Mandala,* a novel permeated with symbolism, both in character
and images, mysticism is an important aspect. But White's concept of

"saint" and "devil" is not that of the ordinary Christian, but more vague; and he shows considerable ambivalence towards Arthur and Mrs. Powler, who are elevated as "saints," and Waldo, who is damned as a "devil."

In the title story, "The Cockatoos," Mick and Olive Davoren have not spoken to one another for seven years; they communicate with each other by writing notes on a pad in the kitchen. They don't have much to say to each other in essential matters. Mick has taken to sometimes having tea with Busby Le Cornu, a spinster up the road, and once in a while their relations have been more intimate, though Mick shows as little enthusiasm for love as he does for talk. The women in this triangle share an interest in music and their not talking about their interests is strange. The catalyst that introduces life and death into this long-standing deadlock is the arrival of a flock of brilliant wild cockatoos. Olive and Mick take turns feeding them, and their shared enthusiasm for the birds leads them to exchange words, and even inarticulate love, for the first time in many years. It is a typical Narayan situation, but White gives it a tragic ending. Mick is shot trying to protect the cockatoos from the neighbour with a shotgun, and the women join hands supporting his dying body. The story has a violent and a melodramatic ending. White's sympathy, sometimes vitiated by a patrician contempt for the herd, is here allowed full scope. There is the sureness of touch of his best work in the spare, compassionate, unsentimental view he takes of his three characters.

The couple in "Sicilian Vespers" seem to be happy with their lot: "Prudence was a virtue normally present in both of them. What had made their marriage such an exceptionally happy one was its balance" (198). Dr. Charles Simpson and his wife Ivy lead superficial lives; they are snobs, and they have no children (like many couples in White). "Five-Twenty" is a tragic story: Ella Natwick delays her protest against the kiss of death represented by her marriage until after her husband has passed on.

In "The Full Belly," hunger drives Costa Iordanou and his elderly aunt Pronoe to violate both religious belief and aristocratic family decorum by fighting over a plate of rice left as a ritual. Athens has been desecrated by the invading Germans, and the Greeks are driven to desecrate their own most cherished tradition in the fight for survival. In "The Cockatoos," nine-year-old Tim Goodenough despairs of making contact with his parents and spends a night in the park; he kills an old cockatoo, one of the Lawrentian life-symbols of the body, hoping that the violent destruction of life will enable him somehow to touch its essence. Desecration and betrayals recur in the stories; and in the degradation that follows them, it is possible (though by no means certain) that the characters will discover their lost humanity. "Willy-wagtails by Moonlight" (In *The Burnt Ones*), has some of the qualities of irony which are close to Narayan's. It briefly and simply surprises the reader into acknowledging that there is more in a dull character than meets the eye — even of his friends. The Wheelers visit the Mackenzies, who are newly rich and still embarrassed about it. They are in time to see Mackenzie's dowdy secretary leaving the house, where she has been helping her boss in running the firm. The Mackenzies entertain their guests with tape-recordings of bird songs they have heard, but still it is a dull evening. Arch Mackenzie cuts his hand in a lamp-globe. His wife asks him to change, and he calls her to attend to the tape-recorder. Correctly sociable in a North Shore way, she plays her guests a tape that she has not heard of willy-wagtails singing at night, while she is out of the room. But as well as the bird-song, it has recorded the drunken reveries of Arch Mackenzie. The wife returns to the room in time to hear the concluding beauties of two bird songs, which is enough to indicate to Mackenzie that his guests have heard more than they should have.

In order that the surprise should work, the story depends on the coincidence of Arch Mackenzie's absence and his wife's choosing just this tape to play. Besides the quality of being psychologically intact, the story exhibits a structural irony: Mrs. Mackenzie offers the characteristically pacifying remark, "A little alcohol releases the vitality." The story suggests one of the limitations of White's sarsaparilla as a microcosm of modern Australia. *The Cockatoos* is a sort of novella in which White attacks crass materialism and the philistine stupor of the Australian scene; he surveys the surface of his life with a caricaturist's eye for the vulgarity of the lamb chop and tomato sauce. This is common in some recent Australian writers like Barry Humphries and David Williamson. In contrast, Randolph Stow, who has left warm Australia for the cold world outside, remembers with sorrow (as well as anger) the warmth he left behind.

The Fazackerleys of "A Woman's Hand" are comfortably off and retired. Evelyn Fazackerley's response to the scene is almost as repulsive as the author's description of it: "How vulgar they all are ... there are certain standards the ones who know can't afford to drop." After such a beginning, reminiscent of Dickensian grotesque, the Fazackerleys live their lives distanced from others. They live in a cosy, tasteful unit very like a prison cell. Into this situation are introduced Clem Dowson and Nesta Pine, school-friends of Harold and Evelyn Fazackerley, who stir vague and poetic longings and are able to relieve some of her anxiety by arranging the poisonous marriage between them. These characters are interesting in detailing routine habits and talking about egg-remover and garbage cans; but we see nothing of their inner life. Clem and Nesta are shadowy, and we see them through the Fazackerleys. White has written about his outsiders with such perception and sensitivity elsewhere that it is hard to accept the mere outlines of these characters.

White's stories are violent: events describe betrayals caused by the eruption of basic human cravings and the indifference of the world and the inadequacy of the institutions of marriage.

To move from White to Narayan is like moving away from trekking in the Sahara to a delightful walk in the garden of Krishnaraja Sagar. We go from a florid, vigorous style to a charming, unobtrusive one. Narayan, on a small canvas, creates characters that are familiar, and even his weaker novels serve as keys to his society, the India of everyday with its familiar Malgudi ethos, the school, the post office, the railway station, and even the cricket team — a colonial gift now popular in all towns and villages of India. Malgudi's Market Road is well laid out with its printing presses and animated torpor of human and animal life, which move about undisturbed, perhaps, by the smell of flowers, fruits and eatables. "What divine sweets the Bombay Ananda Bhavan made!" This makes one's mouth water. Narayan's India becomes familiar as one goes from one story to another and one novel to another; it is like Hardy's Wessex or Dicken's London. One knows the topography of these novelists like the palm of one's hand. Although this familiar milieu has worked against all cult novelists, the readers settle down. In a way, this does not apply to White, whose background and education are different, who writes about a megalomaniac explorer in *Voss* or people pitted against evil in *Riders in the Chariot* or about homosexuals in *The Twyborn Affair* or about the Greeks in *The Burnt Ones*. White moves his characters from continent to continent and from nation to nation; the characters in Narayan have intimacy, assurance, and honesty. His humour and his stories are of the tradition of the

Panchatantra and the *Hitopadesa*: they are didactic and in places downright funny. Humour abounds in a language of vitality and of living expression. In Indian writing in English, humour acquires connotations different from those of the West. If Chesterton's bishop had slipped on a banana-skin in an Indian street, people might attribute it to demonic possession, but they would laugh before rising to help him up.

Narayan's characters are of every day, his novels are comedies of the sort that require a limited social setting with well-defined rules, and "Malgudi is a creation of art." When, in 1963, V.S. Naipaul visited India for the first time, he found that Narayan's novels did not prepare him for "the distress" of India. The reality was cruel and overwhelming. "In the books (Narayan's), India had seemed accessible, in India it remained hidden" (186). This is true of all writers who are concerned with idealised truth in fiction, but distress is not completely absent in Narayan. He is India's most sensitive interpreter. In *The World of Nagaraj* the would-be author is shattered by his discovering that the world is an instrument designed to torment the harmless. Nagaraj is simple; his idea of heaven is to sit on the pyol, observing the world passing; his only ambition is to write a biography of the sage Narada. Narayan's sense of humane balance as a writer never quite lets Nagaraj know that his life is empty — he tortures him with hope. Sometimes a Narayan character seems to be naive but familiar, and he becomes a visionary, as in *The English Teacher,* or a champion of the women's liberation movement, as in *The Dark Room,* or a comic portrayal of the myth of Rakshasa (Bhasmasura) who carries within himself a tiny seed of self-destruction, as in *The Man-Eater of Malgudi.*

Narayan is grateful to India, whose material for short stories is limitless. India is not standardised or mechanised and is free from monotony. His Malgudi stays with him; it stays with him even when he stays in New York. "I can detect Malgudi characters even in New York, for instance, West Twenty-third Street, where I have lived for many months at a time off and on since 1959, possesses every element of Malgudi, with its landmarks and humanity remaining unchanged" (*My Days* 116). His work demonstrates a sanguine acceptance of present-day India. In *Malgudi Days,* he says, "It is stimulating to live in a society that is not standardised or mechanised, and is free from monotony; under such conditions, the writer has only to look out of the window to pick up a character" (ix). Hence, "India will go on." This attitude makes him different from White, who had a love-hate relationship with Australia and who was at times disgusted with his country of breeding dogs and growing vegetables but stayed on to work on a refreshed landscape which even in its shabbier, remembered version always made a background to his life. He loved Greece, but it was Australia that inspired him.

Narayan stories have the brevity and limitations of fables mixed with a certain slickness, imitated, perhaps, from the fiction of those English magazines like the *Strand* and *Mercury*, which, Narayan has told us in his autobiography, *My Days,* entranced his youth and led to his first attempts to write. This is in keeping with his mentor Graham Greene's remark that the children's books which were read in youth have far more effect on writers' subsequent style than critics generally realise. Yet it cannot be fairly said that the author averts his gaze from poverty. Many of the stories deal with people to whom a few rupees — even as little as one rupee a day — means the difference between starvation and survival. "Naga" describes the plight of a boy somewhat more than ten years old whose father, a snake charmer, has abandoned him, leaving him eight paise in small change and a snake too enfeebled by age to impress the street crowds. "No one is afraid of you," the boy tells the snake, "and do you know what that means? I starve, that's all."

Narayan's milieu is the humdrum, philistine world of the average man. The astrologer is a memorable character. "Punctually at midday he opened his bag and spread out his professional equipment, which consisted of a dozen cowrie shells, a square piece of cloth with obscure, mystic charts on it, a notebook, and a bundle of palmyra writing." Those who want to know their future are impressed with his appearance: "his forehead was resplendent with sacred ash and vermilion, and his eyes sparkled with a sharp abnormal gleam which was really an outcome of a continual search for customers, but which his simple clients took to be a prophetic light and felt comforted."

Narayan's tale-telling impulse carries his readers along, providing them with protean variety of incidents, sometimes funny and sometimes sad (as in the case of Ramanujam of *The Mission Mail* and of the Lawley Extension patient who turns the corner in spite of the doctor of "The Doctor's World"). The blind man's insatiable thirst for money and for exploiting the loyalty of the dog in "The Blind Dog" and Rajam Iyer's behaviour in the third-class compartment (in "Fellow Felling"), are realistic pictures. But Iswaran, a character in a story of the same name who passes all examinations like Robert Bruce, is a thick-skinned idiot who forgets his misery by going to a film, "losing himself in politics and struggles of gods and goddesses" and "in the vision of a heavenly world which some film director has chosen to present." He nevertheless allows an imaginary horse to carry him to the Sarayu River and get drowned.

Some of Narayan's stories begin with monologues such as the utterances of the Talkative Man in "The Snake Song," a man playing the flute with such inspiration that the god Nagaraja appears and compels him to play all night long. A certain benign fate guides these characters in their dear little town; their lives are brief and sometimes appear flimsy as, for instance, Raja, the pickpocket of "The Trail of the Green Blazer," who is portrayed very sympathetically. All sorts of characters inhabit Malgudi's teeming streets. "Is there any other place where you can get coffee for six pice and four chappaties for an anna?" asked one of Rama's customers in the Market Corner, soon to be destroyed by hooligans. The author's comment is, "The gods grow jealous of too much contentment anywhere."

Narayan's portraits never go out of date in a country like India. The Ayah of "A Willing Slave," who "received two meals a day, with five children. Kanna, who had not a quarter of an anna anywhere about him, played dice at the Mantapam, losing all the money stolen from his son's box." The piety of the common man is bound into the substance of the characters. Ramy, of "Mother and Son," who could not pass the intermediate examination or earn even twenty rupees, is pressurised by his mother to marry her brother's daughter; he leaves home after dinner in a huff. The mother spends a restless night, lisping the holy name of Sri Rama and imagining that her son may be drowned in Kukkatahalli Tank. Early in the morning she discovers, to her dismay, that he was sleeping on one of the stone benches on the tank side. This story seems to whisper that there is a limit to what we can bear and that sometimes a trivial event can crush us.

There are two stories of animals mixed with human beings as characters. "The Cat and Tiger" probably reminds the readers of *A Tiger for Malgudi*, in which Raja, the tiger, a proud and unmitigated animal, is transformed into a philosopher like one of Blake's songs of innocence moving into a song of experience. In "God and the Cobbler," a lowly street cobbler, a picture of resignation with no longing or regret in his race, believes an American hippie who had flown from bombing missions in Vietnam to be a mendicant, or a god. The hippie had watched Kumbha Mela at Allahabad and seen a sadhu, who had a tiger for company, claiming to be his long-lost brother in a previous birth. The cobbler and the hippie understand each other. The cobbler, who has lost his son and is taking care of his grandson, muses on life and rebirth. On seeing the figure of Durga in the possession of the hippie for whom he has no respect, he says, "Even a god steals when he has a chance." In "Hungry Child," Raman and Daisy of *The Painter of Signs* reappear. Raman accidentally adopts a child who has· strayed away from his parents. When he is about to like him, the child is torn away from him. Raman returns home in the sands of the Sarayu.

In the same poignant mood we meet Rao (alias Emden) of the story "Burden." He is eighty years old, was once a powerful man, and is the father of innumerable children; he has married thrice and now has a mistress. He remembers his salad days of fifty-one years ago. Going in search of his mistress, he buys her *jilabi* sweets, wanders about in search of her house at the cross street, and looks for the house with a coconut palm. He gets confused; streets have disappeared; he cannot trace the house. He feels sad, he pokes his staff into a brown mongrel lying curled in the dust and the packet of *jilabi* slips out of his hands into the mouth of the dog. Like a philosopher, he utters to himself, "Who knows who is perhaps in this incarnation now!" "Emden" is a very great achievement.

Both Narayan and White demonstrate an insistent compassion for those growing old: detached and dissociated feelings belong to the arguing mind. Narayan and White seek and produce beauty in people, places and things, sense of which may be temporarily lost. This is what Keats called "the feel of not to feel it."

India's poor may not bear the burden of a novel but may beautifully fit into the short story. All Narayan's characters, however humble they may be, are complex: they possess a sense of wonder and enjoy the fringes of life. In the stories there is no space to raise fundamental issues; in them the mystery of existence is outside his scope. But his style, simple as it is, embraces layered riches.

Life, as seen by Patrick White and R.K. Narayan in their stories, is quite different: plebeian, lonely, loveless, and painful in White; poor failures, but optimists in Narayan. White works on an epic scale and moves from continent to continent; he is close to Joyce, for he and Joyce hold up a mirror in which the victims may see unpalatable truths about themselves, and if they are not sanguine enough to hope, like Gulliver, for the immediate reform of the country, they do lend moral support to characters like Harold Fazackerly or Maria in Joyce's "Clay," who make their protest, however, feebly, against the stifling of their human needs. As the unravished Felicity Bannister of White's "The Night the Prowler" complains to her passionless fiance, how can love be 'engaged'?.... and how can an engagement be broken? Anything big enough ought to be *shattered* (143). But nothing big enough comes to people in the stories. The very poor and helpless are something of an embarrassment to a novel — not enough happens to them: their struggles are too one-sided and hopeless. But a short story, like the flare of a match, brings human faces out of the darkness and reveals depths beyond statistics. The realities of marriage are harshly portrayed in White. On the other hand, Narayan's interest is to "only connect." Dr Rann of *Talkative Man*, Narayan's latest novel, is married but is not allowed to seduce or abduct a young girl in Malgudi and thus destroy a happy married life.

In 1973, in an interview, White said, "I feel my novels are quite old-fashioned and traditional — almost nineteenth century. I've never thought of myself as an innovator" (Marr 182). He has not added to the radical development of the novel in the twentieth century, although he has put the capacious potential of the Victorian novel to precise and specialised use: his aim was to introduce a new continent into literature. Both Narayan and he are indifferent to the techniques of the new story, the metafictional, post-modernist impression that calls into doubt the old conventions and the old contracts between reader and writer. White's attempt to capture the quintessential nature of the civilisations in a Virgillian manner is praiseworthy. In Narayan, small men seek their own solutions within an insoluble mass that makes other writers despair. His subjects seem to be on the knees of gods, given as a boon. In Narayan's simple stories of poverty and failure and in White's loneliness, the implicit social protest that we feel in such classics as Chekhov's "Grief," O. Henry's "Gift of the Magi," and Flannery O'Connor's "The Artificial Nigger" (to portray poverty or lovelessness) is to cry against them.

All storytellers are in what Mark Twain called the tradition of the Indian grandmother: a venerable tradition of the bland, broadminded grandmother who indulges in "the most beautiful lies...full of surprises, and adventures, and incongruities, and contradictions, and incredibilities" (85). Narayan's social range, and his successful attempt to convey an entire population, in a way comes close to White's epic magnitude. Their methods stem from their different backgrounds — one a believer without any formal faith and the other an orthodox brahmin of Vedic background. However, there is in both a vivid rendering of characters and continents: in White, Greece becomes a symbol of the possibilities of redemption through beauty and intense passion, just as Italy does for E.M. Forster and Malgudi for R.K. Narayan. In White, angst and loneliness dominate; in Narayan, cheer and hope pervade; one is serious and the other seemingly facetious.

The main pleasure that one gets from reading these short stories of contrast is that of temporarily inhabiting a world different from our own yet connected with it, so that it throws light on the life that we live and on the nature of the people we know, or even just meet. This helps to reveal ourselves, as Milton put it, "in our wonder and astonishment."

Works Cited

Marr, David. *Patrick White: A Biography*. New York: Random, 1991.

Naipaul, V.S. *India: A Wounded Civilization*. New York: Vintage, 1978.

Narayan, R.K. *Malgudi Days: Short Stories*. London: Heinemann, 1982.

—, *My Days: A Memoir*. New Delhi: Orient, 1986.

——, *Talkative Man*. New York: Viking, 1987.

Twain, Mark. *Following the Equator*. New York: Harper, 1897.

White, Patrick. *The Burnt Ones*. New York: Viking, 1964.

—, *The Cockatoos: Stories*. London: Cape, 1974.

—, *Flaws in the Glass: A Self-Portrait*. London: Cape, 1981.

7

THE INTRIGUING VOICE OF R.K. NARAYAN

SITA KAPADIA

(College of Staten Island : City University of New York)

Among writers writing in English anywhere, R.K. Narayan has a distinctive voice. A lively storyteller, he sprinkles his tales with humour but withholds the derisive sting; while he is engagingly realistic in his descriptions, his words are not cut-and-dry; while he vividly portrays the failings and foibles of his townsfolk he never fails to extend to them his humane indulgence. He draws to his writing the stalwart literary critic as well as the undergraduate student of literature; he engages the sophisticated and the discerning as well as the casual, untutored reader. The voice of such a person, the voice of such a writer, is naturally intriguing.

What is the basis for this voice? How is it created? Narayan himself may have the best answers to these questions, if he chooses to engage in the necessary vivisection. To me, it is an engrossing subject — engrossing because challenging, and a challenge worth taking up because it yields richer than usual rewards. Voice, in literature, may be defined as an elusive and distinctive combination of a certain preferred syntax, a choice of words, a pattern of rhythms, and an attitude towards the reader and the world. Voice, in a singer, is resonance in sound; all singers do not have it. Narayan does have it, and it has long captivated me; finally, I can say I have uncovered its likely source.

Webster's New Universal Unabridged Dictionary offers a succcinct and pertinent dictionary definition of *voice:* "the characteristic speech sounds normally made by a certain person." We know the voices of familiar people on the telephone before they say who they are. This is because each person has a voice as distinctive as fingerprints. When the term "voice" is applied to written literature, it signifies the characteristic speech sounds conveyed through writing. A writer, however, may not be as easily identified unless he is eminently distinctive. This is so because (beyond the literal, obvious subject matter) writing conveys emotional and philosophic meaning. As John Dewey says, "Poets and philosophers may democratically share accent and rhythm as ways of shaping communication" (78). Our author is both poet and philosopher by virtue of his shaping voice.

This shaping quality comes from the voice of the storyteller, who speaks in the rhythms of everyday speech, the natural iambic rhythm, direct and comfortable, marking the interactions of real persons with their real surroundings. The natural tempo, following by and large the basic syntax of English (the subject-verb-object order), places events authentically in the rhythm of life. Unlike the periodic sentence, with its limited academic appeal, and the cumulative sentence, with its artful rhetoric, it imparts immediacy and easy intimacy to the writing and thereby creates a bond between the writer and his readers.

Further, the fluid interaction engendered by natural rhythm is enhanced by Narayan's "real voice." In *Writing with Power,* the most imaginative and extensive study that explores voice, Peter Elbow says that real voice comes from real self. Real voice has liveliness and energy, as well as power and resonance. Adding to this idea, Elbow says, "I see that when people start using their real voice, it tends to start them on a trend of growth and empowerment in their way of using words — empowerment even in relating to people" (245). I believe Narayan has the spontaneous intimacy with his reader that comes from such empowerment.

His bond with the reader strengthens because he writes about the living world he witnesses. The subjects of Narayan's works may best be described in his own words: "The material available to a story writer in India is limitless. Within a broad climate of inherited culture there are endless variations: every individual differs from every other individual, not only economically, but in outlook, habits and day-to-day philosophy.

It is stimulating to live in a society that is not standardised or mechanised, and is free from monotony" (*Malgudi* iii). Though Narayan is speaking here in the context of the difference between the arduous task of crafting a novel and simply looking out of a window and picking up a story, what he says about the individual and freedom from monotony holds true of characters in his novels as well.

Finding out all about his characters, with their individual idiosyncrasies, he does not feel the need to invent the absurd, to promote social theory, to seek sensational subjects, or to delve into abnormal psychology to get his reader's attention or to be regarded as a writer of consequence. It takes a great deal of courage and self-possession in a writer — especially a modern writer — to write about ordinary, everyday occurrences in the lives or ordinary, everyday people; it takes a great deal of talent and truth to keep the reader interested in and enthralled by such writing, story after story, book after book. It must take more than syntax, word choice, presentation of ideas, or some underfined expectation to keep interest mounting. I think it has to do with the writer's voice. We want to listen to him, to his voice.

The spoken charm or oral quality of Narayan's writing is unmistakable. Most of it comes to us in first-person narrative. Whether it be poignant nostalgia, sombre recollection, self-justifying reverie, compulsive talk, or comical recounting, it has the intimacy of the talking voice. It is distinctly not the voice of a distant and stern adjudicator of human predicament; rather, it is confiding, spontaneous — as though unedited, full of warmth and verve.

Furthermore, Narayan's world is very much like the world of his storyteller in *Gods, Demons, and Others:*

> Everything is interrelated. Stories, scriptures, ethics, philosophy, grammar, astrology, astronomy, semantics, mysticism, and moral codes — each is part and parcel of total life and is indispenasable for the attainment of a four-square understanding of existence. Literature is not a branch of study to be placed in a separate compartment, for the edification only of scholars, but a comprehensive and artistic medium of expression to benefit the literate and the illiterate alike (xi-xii).

In the world of the imagination, if it is necessary to have a prerequisite (the willing suspension of disbelief), then in Narayan's imaginatively recreated world of real, everyday characters there is another given: the willing suspension of harsh indictment. This is not to say that there is no moral or intellectual discrimination as to the chasm between the saint and the scoundrel; it is, in fact, keenly present, but dispensed with clarity, homour, and faith that the scoundrel — and even savage — may someday become a saint. Raju, the unscrupulous guide, with holiness thrust upon him, does become a caring, self-sacrificing saviour. The once-wild tiger, becoming a non-violent sojourner in Malgudi, is assured of *moksha* (salvation). This is not a pattern in Narayan's novels, though, for there are others that remain incorrigibly greedy, habitually deceptive. The imposter Dr. Rann (in *Talkative Man*) and Sampath (in *Mr. Sampath*) are two such irreversibles.

There is, then, not a pattern in plot that gives resonant voice to Narayan's writing but a pattern of faith. I believe that it is worth exploring the content of Narayan's work by applying the "neti, neti" (not this, not this) method of negation in Indian metaphysics to discover the truth. Many a nineteenth - and twentieth-century writer of eminence points a finger at society for the evil that men do. Dostoevsky's protagonist in *Crime and Punishment*, outraged at a society that robs people of human dignity, becomes a murderer. Apparently no such thesis underlies Narayan's plots; nor is there an existential finger waving about, exposing absurdity, the meaninglessness of life. Narayan does not perplex. We do not tease our minds as we do with Albert Camus over the senseless actions in *The Stranger* or cogitate with Franz Kafka about *The Metamorphosis* or wonder why a whole village in Japan shovels sand all night, every night, in Kobo Abe's *Woman in the Dunes*. Narayan's characters do not stand for anything other than themselves, individuals free of the monotony of modernisation and standardisation.

A variety of issues (modernisation, Westernisation, caste, prejudice, violence, urban dehumanisation, oppresssion of women, injustice, and many more) form part of the human drama energising the story. But nowhere, not even in *A Painter of Signs* or *The Dark Room,* does the theme (feminism, in these two novels?) overshadow the story. And the story is not an excuse for sizzling social issues as we often find in the novels of Kamala Markandaya or Chinua Achebe or Buchi Emecheta, nor for imaginative predictions of the future as in the works of Isaac Asimov. But social awareness and vivid imagination are ever-present in the very tone and turn of phrase of the narrative.

For instance, Srinivas brings up the matter of Sampth's affair:

At first Sampath pooh-poohed the entire story. But later said, with
his old mischievous look coming back to his eyes : "Some people
say that every sane man needs two wives — a perfect one for the
house and a perfect one for outside social life .... I have the one,
why not the other? I have confidence that I will keep both of them
happy and if necessary in separate houses. Is a man's heart so
narrow that it cannot accommodate more than one? I have married
according to Vedic rites: let me have one according to the civil
marriage law...." (179)

What I see running through Narayan's work is a pattern of faith.
In *Swami and Friends* it was intuited. It became explicit in *My Days:
A Memoir* and in *The English Teacher* (alternatively titled *Grateful to
Life and Death,* a title that bears significance to all of Narayan's work).
The boy in the memoir, more at ease with the peacock and the monkey
than with other boys, grows up into a young man steeped in literature,
with a preference for reading and writing at Kukkanhalli Tank to
teaching some meaningless things by rote to uninterested schoolboys.
An absence of worldly wisdom, a pervasive listlessness, as well as an
emptiness, seems to hover over his life, even when he is seemingly
happily married. It is only after his wife's death, when he is intuitively
drawn to the life of spiritual living, that he finds fulfilment in non-
attachment, sacrifice, and service, maturing thus far beyond his earlier
self-absorption. He accepts circumstances with peace in his heart, grateful
to life and death. A close parallel to this memoir is evident in *The
English Teacher.* Perhaps not so obviously, but similarly and subtly in
every story, whether there is a radical transformation or not, a movement,
a magnetic pull, toward the spiritual is discernible. Religion is not a
theme; it is not even obliquely presented through Narayan's characters
or zealously debated by them. However, a strong spirituality, a Hindu
awareness, is latent. *The Vendor of Sweets* begins with an apparently
flippant remark by the universal cousin about giving up over-fondness
for food; the essence of the novel is the resilience of a broken paternal
heart that learns non-attachment, letting go, and contemplation. It is as
central to the Hindu way was anything can be. It is the premise of
many a Narayan novel that, even when not explicitly stated, informs
the argument or the core of the story. It resonates clearly in *A Tiger
for Malgudi, The Financial Expert, The Guide* and *The Vendor of
Sweets.* The choice of subject is an index. In the *Ramayana,* the incarnate

Rama is goodness itself, but whereas he is not always infallible, he is always endearing, And there is a significant connection between character portrayal and the voice of the writer, for the voice expresses philosophy and faith, thought and feeling.

Many of Narayan's stories are recollections of the protagonists; they are narrations that express the quiet wisdom of hindsight. This is radically different from the time-reversed, attention-grabbing technique of plunging headlong into the fray at a point of conflict, developing a complication, and manoeuvring a resolution. Not so the voice of reveries, which is couched in the attitude of live-and-let-live. In "Uncle," the little boy's attachment to Uncle and his growing awareness of the sinister history of that adored elder is told from the contentment and comfort of an easy chair. The narrator is himself the beneficiary, the inheritor of Uncle's presumably wicked spoils. As a young man supported by apparently the most gentle of souls, the God-loving, plant-cultivating imposter, he dispenses with moral issues with convenient speed. When he tells the story, he is indolent, indulgent, and certainly not given to either self-doubt or self-blame; it is the voice of calm-of-mind-all passions-spent. The voice of torture is absent; the voice of philosophy is low-key but strong. It is typical of Narayan. It explains, partly, the importance of "Uncle"; the ambivalence of the genre label (short novel or long short story), to which our author is probably quite indifferent, is symptomatic of the freedom from moral dogma. All comes from a place in peace.

Literature must at once entertain and uplift. Narayan never loses his hold on those perennial essentials of great literature. The story is primary; we clamour for more, more! In terms of outer action, the stories are simply and traditionally crafted. The progression is generally chronological and often presented as events recollected by the protagonist. The English teacher, Raju, TM, the nephew in "Uncle" are some of them. While there is a deliberate self-awareness on their part, there is not the rush and plunge, and back-swirl of the stream of consciousness. The narrative moves along naturally, as though effortlessly in a quiet yet lively tempo of natural (by which I mean oral) expression. Reading any page, even a randomly opened page of Narayan's writing, assures the reader that wit and style are not lost but enthrallingly present. Here are the opening lines from *Talkative Man:*

They call me Talkative Man. Some affectionately shorten it to TM: I have earned this title, I suppose, because I cannot contain myself.

My impulse to share an experience with others is irresistible, even if they sneer at my back, I don't care. I'd choke if I didn't talk...perhaps like Sage Narada of our epics, who for all his brilliance and accomplishments carried a curse on his back that unless he spread a gossip a day, his skull would burst." (1)

Who can resist reading on? Who is not enchanted by the wit and style, the ambiance of his words?

Every page delights the reader. From Susila's two-digit accounting in "Grateful to Life and Death" to the half-uttered, oblique and inconclusive dialogues between Nagaraj and his wife Sita in *The World of Nagaraj,* we read and keep reading and want more. Why? It is, perhaps, because they provide present comfort to our own uneventful mental joggings on the spot, our own seemingly momentous though philosophically inconsequential involvements in our own world. The reason, however, is neither the comfort nor the empathy it provides; it is located in the voice.

There are two basic modes, two generic voices in Narayan's writing: the first person and the third person. The first is intimate, confiding, explicating and self-indulgent. The third person, radically different in theory, is objective, omnisciently commanding a cosmic picture. There is between them the usual intellectual and emotional difference, but essentially a vital concurrence of spirit. The omniscient voice — wiser, brighter, more sophisticated — is none the less just as indulgent, tolerant of human weakness and individual peculiarities as any self-aware and self-absolving first-person oration.

I give below one example of each of these two voices. The first person is beautifully used in this passage from *The Guide:*

The gentle singing in the bathroom ceased; my mother dropped the subject and went away as Rosie emerged from her bath fresh and blooming.... She was completely devoted to my mother. But unfortunately my mother, for all her show of tenderness, was beginning to stiffen inside. She had been listening to gossip, and she could not accommodate the idea of living with a tainted woman. I was afraid to be cornered by her and took care not to face her alone. But whenever she could get at me, she hissed a whisper in my ear, "She is a real snake-woman, I tell you. I never liked her from the first moment you mentioned her." (135-36)

The third person is also well illustrated from the same novel: He felt enraged at the persistence of food-thoughts. With a sort of vindicitive resolution he told himself, "I'll chase away all thought of food. For the next ten days I shall eradicate all thoughts of tongue and stomach from my mind...." Lack of food gave him a peculiar floating feeling, which he rather enjoyed, with the thought in the background, "This enjoyment is something Velan cannot take away from me." (212)

There is here a crucial connection, a vital unity of voice that is more significant than the difference in narrative standpoints.

Again, within the third-person narrative, typically and intimately, the reader comes upon the internal monologue, "the internal controversy" as it is called in *The Bachelor of Arts*, in which Chandran argues with himself:

Chandran steadily discouraged this sceptical half of his mind, and lent his whole-hearted support to the other half....His well-ironed chocolate tweed was sure to invite notice. He hoped that he didn't walk clumsily in front of her. He again told himself she must have noticed that he was not like the rest of the crowd. And so why should he not now go and occupy a place that would be close to her and in direct line of her vision? Staring was half the victory in love. His sceptical half now said that by this procedure he might scare her off the river for ever.... (60)

Further, along with these fictional voices resonates the voice of the writer of *My Days*: "The postman became a source of hope at a distance and of despair when he arrived. My interest in him continues even today. In every country I visit I habitually watch the postman. It's probably a conditioined reflex, like Pavlov's salivating dog." (67)

John Knowles's protagonist, Gene Forrester, in *A Separate Peace*, says, "I knew what I said was important and right and my voice found that full tone voices have when they are expressing something long-felt and long-understood and released at last" (182). R.K. Narayan has that full-tone voice expressing something long-felt and long-understood. Coming thus from a contemplation in the heart as well as the head, it is spiritually mature, free of hatred, contention, resistance, unrest, indignation — howsoever righteous. All one mode or another of reaction to the world, it comes out of wholeness and wholesomeness; it simply tells a story; it tells it with wisdom; it tells it as *leela*.

The writer is a compassionate and joyful witness; what he writes about is the spectacle of life, simply as spectacle, as *leela*, the spontaneous play of the impersonal Being in the universe. It is another way of saying that this is writing without a bias: no urgent need to drive home a point of view, no bitterness, no nostalgia, no anger, no anxiety, no socio-psycho convolutions, no talisman, and no utopia. Perhaps this is the reason Americans, with their overwhelming civil rights consciousness, their constant vigil to guard personal freedom, find Narayan so refreshingly unique, so purely entertaining. Through his writing many a reader, especially many an undergraduate student, has come to understand and love India, its colours and flavours, its variegated humanity who have a local habitation and a name in Malgudi as well as a universal habitation in the minds and hearts and experiences of people everywhere.

The speaking voice is all-important to Narayan himself. He said in *My Days* of Keats, Shelley, Byron, and Browning: "They spoke of an experience that was real and immediate in my surroundings and stirred in me a deep response" (58). The same is true of himself for us. He, too, evokes in us a deep response by speaking to us of the real and the immediate in that voice that comes from the centre.

Peter Elbow says, "Often words from the center are quiet. Their power comes from inner resonance....I would point to the central characteristic of real voice: the words somehow issue from the writer's center... and produce reasonance which gets the words more powerfully to the reader's center" (296).

What a multitude of characters come to mind when we think of Narayan's writing! How engaging are their voices in memoirs, stories and novels! The resonance that comes from witnessing and delighting in life's *leela* comes from the centre. It makes of all these intriguing voices one real voice. It is an endearing voice, the voice of R.K. Narayan himself.

Works Cited

Dewey, John. *Art as Experience*. Ed. Jo Ann Boydstom. New York: Minton, 1934.

Elbow, Peter. *Writing with Power*. New York: Oxford UP, 1981.

Knowles, John. *A Separate Peace*. New York: Bantam, 1959.

Narayan, R.K. *The Bachelor of Arts*. Mysore: Indian Thought, 1987.

—, *Gods, Demons, and Others.* New York: Bantam, 1986.

—, *The Guide.* New York: Viking, 1958.

—, *Malgudi Days.* New York: Viking, 1982.

—, *Mr. Sampath.* Mysore: Indian Thought, 1956.

—, *My Days: A Memoir.* New York: Viking, 1982.

—, *Talkative Man.* Mysore: Indian Thought, 1986.

8

THE COMEDY OF MISREADING IN THE FICTION OF R.K. NARAYAN

SUSAN LEVER
(Australian Defence Force Academy)

In Joseph Furphy's Australian novel *Such is Life,* the narrator meets a boundary rider living with his wife and daughter in the isolated west of New South Wales. Rory O'Halloran has difficulty identifying the few trees in his paddock but impresses the narrator with his expertise on the Presidents of the United States and the laying of the transatlantic telegraph cable. When the narrator visits Rory's hut, he finds that his only reading matter is a dictionary, a Bible, a complete works of Shakespeare and an 1865 volume of *Macmillan's Magazine.* Of course, this volume of *Macmillan's* includes articles on the American Presidents and the transatlantic telegraph. Though Rory is not on speaking terms with his own wife, with the help of the dictionary he has written a perfectly spelt treatise on Woman, based on a comparison of the women of the Bible and Shakespeare's heroines.

Furphy's character serves as a salutory example to all critics who are about to embark on an interpretative essay: there is nothing more absurd than the expert who does not allow limited information about his or her subject to interfere with a theory that claims to comprehend all aspects of the matter in hand. This lesson must be taken to heart, particularly by the critic who wishes to offer a paper on a writer from another culture. In a sense, of course, we are all Rory O'Hallorans interpreting the universe on the basis of the few aspects of it that have attracted our attention. But an Australian critic, like myself, reading the fiction of an Indian writer such as R.K. Narayan ought to be aware that sheer ignorance may create certain comic pitfalls— that the task of critical interpretation may well become a comic role.

When Western critics write about the work of Narayan, they are likely to mention the way in which he has made the English language and a European literary form, the novel, seem Indian—at least, to Western readers. They are likely to comment that Narayan's achievements lie in the use of one cultural medium to convey the atmosphere of a quite different culture. They might be inclined to marvel, too, that Narayan's Indian fiction seems not so much exotic as familiar to readers from these different cultures— as if some kind of conjuring trick has occurred whereby Malgudi and its people are as recognisable as, say, London and its streets. Sita Kapadia's account of her American students reading Narayan confirms that this Western response to the fiction is widespread.

Nevertheless, it surprises me that many readers who know nothing about India feel confident that they understand what Narayan says to them and are not assailed by doubts that they may be misreading. At the most, there may be some hesitancy about the moments when Narayan's writing leaves the unconventional realist account of experience, those religious or mystical moments when his characters are lifted out of the everyday world by some intimation of a greater existence—for example, when the vendor of sweets crosses the river under the guidance of the image-maker or the man-eater of Malgudi emerges as more demon than man. But these moments can be shrugged off as part of the exotic Indian culture. It is, I suppose, an expected difference rather than a challenging one.

Somehow, Narayan convinces his foreign readers that they have the power to read the signs he offers them. So it is all the more surprising that, often, his characters fail to understand the messages they give each other. The comedy in Narayan's fiction is often a comedy of misunderstanding; in particular, a failure of one character to read the language of another or a regarding of that language which is ultimately fanciful to the point of absurdity. Misreading is everywhere in Narayan's fiction, and I want to argue that it operates within several frames: that not only is the subject of the fiction often the misreading of events and characters by another character, but that Narayan also presents the writer as a reader (and possibly misreader) of event and character, and that, at the outer frame, the reader of Narayan's fiction would do well to acknowledge the incompleteness of any reading of the text.

Let me begin by describing the way in which misreading serves two of Narayan's best-known stories, "A Horse and Two Goats" and "An Astrologer's Day," which are included in *Under the Banyan Tree.* In "A Horse and Two Goats" a poor and very old Tamil peasant sits by the roadside tending his goats when a passing American's van runs out of gas. The American decides that he wants to buy the mud horse under which Muni sits. After quelling his initial fears, Muni believes that the American wants some conversation and then that he wishes to buy the two goats. Muni speaks in Tamil, the American in English, and they misinterpret gestures as well as speech. The obvious clash comes from the two cultures—Muni being the poorest member of the tiniest village in India, the American being a New Yorker whose immediate problem is gas for his car.

In this story the American's assumptions about Muni and the horse are based on stereotypes of the exotic, while Muni has sat under the horse so long and known its history so much that he cannot see it as a desirable (or saleable) piece of property. On the other hand, Muni's immediate reaction to the Westerner is to regard him as a figure of authority. The story, I think, offers some gentle criticism of the American while it laughs at both characters. The American talks about technology (power failures and television sets), and he interprets Muni's account of the history of the horse as "sales talk". The surprising thing is that despite the fact that the Western reader of this story knows the world of the American best, she or he will be inclined to see the encounter through Muni's perspective. Because Narayan carefully builds up an understanding of the details of life for the Tamil peasant, we are forced to look at this American with new eyes; in effect, to look at ourselves and our own assumptions. Yet the story does not satirise Westerners. It suggests that the misunderstandings are based on an essential goodwill and a common inability to control the conditions of life; after all, the American has come to India because a power strike on the hottest day in New York has sent him to look at another civilisation. Even Westerners are not immune to the failure of technology.

In "An Astrologer's Day," the astrologer earns his living by reading the lives of others— a skill based on listening to their talk; but his great coup comes at the moment when he manages to read the life of the man he once tried to kill, while remaining safe in his role of astrologer. In this case, the ability to read conveys power and protection to the accurate reader, while the misreader can be sent away harmless. In this case the astrologer is most obviously a reader; but if he also appears to adopt a role like that of the writer, or storyteller, then that seems an appropriate image to Narayan's approach to writing. For it is possible to see him as teaching us to read the mysteries of other lives.

There are numerous other examples of this pattern of reading and misreading in the short stories; but rather than list them, I would like to draw attention to two first-person stories where the figure who struggles to read and never quite grasps the complete meaning of the signs, is the narrator, an autobiographical version of Narayan himself. In "Annamalai" the narrator gives a history of his servant patterned around a series of postcards from the servant's village. Typically, the postcards begin with elaborate tidings of well-being and prayer, only to end with a message of disaster and a plea for help. Annamalai knows that the relationship between events and words is a mysterious one and should not be taken for granted. He advises the narrator not to display his name in public and is careful not to speak his own name unnecessarily. The literate narrator has difficulty interpreting the postcard messages for the illiterate Annamalai, and it seems that literacy gives him a different relationship to the world. Yet he recognises that Annamalai's realities — his family's problems in the village with sheep and sewing machines — have a meaning that cannot be fully explained in terms of legal documents or postcards. In this story, once again, the character who is most like the reader in technological knowledge and literacy has most difficulty in reading the signs.

In "A Breath of Lucifer," in the same collection of stories, the narrator's difficulty in understanding or reading the life of another character (in this case the nurse, Sam) is dramatised by his lack of sight. Narayan tells us in a prologue that this story is based on his own experiences after an operation on his eyes. Here, the narrator is dependent on Sam until the bandages on his eyes can be removed. Everything he knows and can tell us about Sam comes from voices and interpretations of voices. The narrator tells us, "Perhaps if I could have watched his facial expressions and gestures I might have understood or interpreted his worlds differently, but in my unseeing state I had to accept literally whatever I heard" (106).

The attendant seems a miracle of helpfulness and kindness —
disappearing and returning instantly with coffee, solicitous over every
aspect of his patient's care. But the narrator can never get him to
reveal the factual details of the stories he tells: Which war did he serve
in? In which campaign did a particular feat of bravery occur? Sam's
stories operate on a level above such authenticating detail. At last,
Sam's decision to celebrate both his own birthday and the removal of
the patient's bandages ends in a new revelation about Sam. His scrupulous
modesty disappears under the influence of alcohol, and the narrator
finds himself led out of the hospital into unfamiliar surroundings,
while Sam appears to have entered completely into his war fantasies,
with the narrator playing the part of a wounded man.

The narrator of this story is literally at the mercy of his character
and, at the end, has become a character of Sam's fantasies. And the
narrator is inclined towards fantasy, too. In his blindness, he imagines
himself walking through strange geological formations, pillars of rock,
or mounds of cotton wool. In this story, the pattern of Narayan's
narrator being a flawed reader of signs is more obvious than in other
stories. The blind narrator tells us not only what he knows but the
limitations of that knowledge. As readers, we must trust our guide; but
that guide, we are told, can never know the full meaning of what he
tells.

"A Breath of Lucifer" is a comic story. Sam's account of his own
likeness to Errol Flynn, or his congratulation of his patient for his tidy
use of the W.C., and even the disappearing drunken voice singing "Has
she got lovely cheeks? Yes, she has lovely cheeks" are very funny. Yet
it is also a story which suggests a dark side to the situation — the
"Breath of Lucifer" of the title. Where, in a story such as "Annamalai,"
the narrator is in control of his own life if not that of his servant, in
"Breath of Lucifer" he is physically vulnerable. And imaginatively he
is vulnerable, too. His vision of an immense pillar in his way suggests
lewd carvings to Sam, so that the characters seem to be entering into
each other's nightmares — one a result of blindness, the other from
drunkenness. The story reveals that there are other modes, besides the
comic, in which misreading can occur. Where the comedy in a story
such as "A Horse and Two Goats" or "Annamalai" my come from the
different levels of knowledge which the reader or characters possess,
"A Breath of Lucifer" recognises that a sense of security in that knowledge
(however meagre or misplaced) allows us a comic perspective. It is

when we feel that matters have gone beyond our control that darker ideas impinge.

I want to read this story as an image of the reader/writer relationship. The reader is as blind as the narrator being led by Sam. We must trust Narayan — just as the narrator trusts Sam — but it is a very uncertain trust. What if Narayan is a liar, a drunkard, or a guide with a diseased imagination? The surprising aspect of Narayan's fiction is that we *do* trust him — that this very declaration of the limits of his own narration wins us. This is partly why Western readers feel so confident in Narayan's hands: India may be a mystery to us, but it is also a mystery to Narayan. He draws our attention to his problems of misreading so that our own are not debilitating.

Narayan's novel *The Vendor of Sweets* plays off misreadings of various kinds to achieve its comedy. The principal difficulty, of course, arises out of Jagan's inability to read his son, Mali. The differences between them come not simply from their ages, their educations, and their philosophies but also their perspectives on the world. And both Jagan and Mali have aspirations to be writers: Jagan's book *Nature Cure and Natural Diet* has been awaiting publication by Nataraj for years, and Mali tells his father that he is going to America to become a writer of novels. It is worth noting how often Narayan's characters are writers (or storytellers) of one kind or another, because it is a sign of Narayan's self-consciousness about his own techniques: a novelist who creates a monosyllabic poet as he does in *The Man Eater of Malgudi* cannot be unaware of the formal demands of his craft.

When Mali returns from the United States with a plan to manufacture a story machine, we might think that the novel has moved into the bounds of the ridiculous. But we can also see this story-writing machine as one of Narayan's images for the whole difficulty of reading and knowing the world. It is the moment when the novel seems to leave the familiar limits of realism behind; and it is also the moment when, I think, Narayan warns his readers that he also is a storyteller and cannot be held to the limitations of the obvious, known world.

The story machine has four knobs — for characters, plot situations, climax and (the fourth knob) to find the right combination of these three and emotions. Characters are "good, bad, neutral"; emotions comprise "love, hate, revenge, devotion, pity," and so on. It is a wonderful joke for a writer whose characters simply do not operate to these simplicities — and a warning for the critic who wants to analyse Narayan's fiction into similar categories. If we need further evidence for Narayan's distrust of such mechanical approaches to literature, we might note that his essay "A Writer's Nightmare" speculates along similar lines about a government ministry of story-writing.

In *The Vendor of Sweets* the reader shares Jagan's perplexity and doubts about the story machine and begins to abandon sympathy for Mali, whose view of the world is fundamentally mechanical and materialistic. We also learn that Grace has been the author of the postcards that Jagan has treasured as signs of his son's interest and concern in his well-being. Writing can be lies; stories can be misleading rather than insights into truth.

There are other indications about the nature of reading in the novel. Jagan reads the *Bhagavad Gita* in his shop each day, even telling his staff that "There is no such thing as reading this book finally; it is something to be read all one's life" (73); he relies for information on out-of-date reports like *Poverty and Un-British Rule in India,* and his commitment to "Nature and the Nature Cure" stems from hearing the "word" from Gandhi in 1937. Jagan's bits and pieces of knowledge come together in a worldview that is both well-meaning and mistaken — his suggested cure for his wife's brain tumour appears cruelly inadequate, and his concern for simplicity does not prevent him from presiding over a successful sweets business. But we sympathise with Jagan's attempt to read the world and his confusion when so many false messages are offered to him by his son.

After Jagan's experiments in price-cutting his sweets, he meets the image-maker/hair-dyer who takes him to the garden on the other side of the river. At this point in the novel, Jagan prepares to change from a maker of sweets and a gatherer of money into something else, to enter on a new life. The problem of the novel, the gap between a son and father, is not resolved by the events or activities of the characters; instead, it is accepted by Jagan as being irreparable. As well, he accepts his own inability to teach the world about pure water, spinning one's own cloth, reading the *Bhagavad Gita,* and so on.

There are two characters in the novel who serve to represent two kinds of greater understanding than Jagan's and whose advice Jagan accepts. The first is the wonderful cousin, who is a great reader of other people, managing to live entirely from his abilities as a flatterer and adviser on practical matters. He is a man of the business world, the commercial world of Malgudi. The second, of course, is the hair-dyer who was once an image-maker — and the cousin warns Jagan of this man's danger to enterprise. The second figure is rather more insubstantial than any other character in the novel. His appearance seems to introduce a supernatural element to the realistic fiction of the earlier part of the novel, and it may seem that it is changing its terms as the crisis of misunderstanding is resolved not by confrontation, reconciliation, or mutual enlightenment for Jagan and Mali but by Jagan's decision to move to another level of existence, a level at which his concern for the world — his business, his money, his ideas for implementing the Mahatma's precepts — no longer matters. At this point, it is as if the novelist is bridging two kinds of fiction as well as two levels of existence.

Yet this supernatural element is not out of keeping with Narayan's comedy of misreading, for the most difficult signs to read in his fiction are those that come from the world beyond the physical senses. In other stories, characters are beset by worries about the astrologer's predictions for wedding days or by changes in the weather and what they portend. We all may have difficulty in reading other people, but reading the signs of that great drama beyond our control is a humbling experience for everyone — even the masterful reader of people and novelist.

And the problem of interpreting signs from the gods leads to argument and irresolution, which places all of Narayan's characters (including his narrators) in a comic universe. His characters may seize, as Jagan does, on one message from the sacred books, or from Gandhi, but fail to take into account other contradictory signs. Even when in the realm of the supernatural on the other side of the river, Jagan and the hair-dyer discuss tax and its difficulties and we are told that, for all his scrupulousness about his staff, or his diet, Jagan has an "habitual, instinctive and inexplicable uneasiness concerning any tax. If Gandhi had said somewhere, 'Pay your sales tax uncomplainingly,' he would have followed his advice, but Gandhi had made no reference to the sales tax anywhere to Jagan's knowledge."(83)

In *The Vendor of Sweets* Narayan does not offer us enlightenment through the perspective of Jagan, as one can imagine some Western writers attempting to do. Jagan remains a flawed human being, just as unable to fathom the mysteries of human nature as he was at the beginning. He does not give up his responsibilities to the material world of commerce and ordinary life but merely changes the balance so that the spiritual world will claim more of his attention. He does, of course, leave Mali to sort out his own problems and recognises in him a spoilt boy — and that is in itself an achievement. But the novel does not follow a pattern of crisis and redemption; the novelist does not have an answer to the puzzles of human relationships any more than Jagan's theories of natural cure can save the life of his wife. We are not dealing here with the Western, possibly Christian, realist tradition in which central characters learn some moral lesson or receive some spiritual insight through experience. In Narayan's novel the novelist can read only so far and no further, because he, too, is part of the comedy of incomplete understanding.

To the Western reader, some of Narayan's stories may seem artless accounts of the novelist's experiences among his fellow-inhabitants of Mysore/Malgudi. They may treasure them as transparent accounts of Indian life, as Graham Greene put it, of "what it is like to be Indian." Though I would not wish to deny the pleasure that the fiction brings to readers who accept it in this way, one should also take due note of the frequency with which the metaphor of misreading is offered to us. Narayan is a writer who presents himself as the reader of character and events, but the meaning of these events and characters is not always clear. We are all, he suggests, likely to misunderstand and misinterpret not only each other but the meaning of the world beyond our immediate experience, including (and especially) the world of the supernatural.

Narayan has expressed distrust for academic approaches to literature, particularly mechanical ones along the lines of the story-writing machine. One can imagine the novelist being suspicious, or at least bemused, by the idea of an academic conference about his work. Critics can, however, take heart from the numerous invitations in his fiction to be wary and critical readers. The many writers and misreaders in his fiction signal to us that we are all participating in a comedy of incomplete knowledge.

Works Cited

Narayan, R.K. *An Astrologer's Day and Other Stories.* Mysore: I n d i a n
    Thought, 1960.

—, *Under the Banyan Tree and Other Stories.* London: Heinemann, 1985.

—, *The Vendor of Sweets.* London: Penguin, 1967.

—, *A Writer's Nightmare: Selected Essays 1958-1988.* New Delhi: Penguin,
    1988.

9

R.K. NARAYAN: THE MALGUDISATION
OF REALITY

SUDESH MISHRA
(University of the South Pacific)

I have, for a number of years now, mulled over V.S. Naipaul's devastating assessment of R.K. Narayan in his book *India: A Wounded Civilization.* In a few pages of limpid prose, Naipaul accuses Narayan of writing cosy novels in which stock figures resolve their piffling traumas in neatly circumscribed settings. Narayan is charged with subscribing to a *karmic* worldview, seen as an ideological retreat for Hindus unable to cope with quotidian realities, afraid of taking action *here* lest it compromise some fundamental principle of metempsychosis. The present, then, must be ridden out, not acted on, for fear that it may jeopardise future incarnations, transgress laws of predestination. Narayan, we are told, shirks responsbility for the manifested world by seeing it through the lens of religion; his is a canonised reality based on the doctrine of withdrawal and quietism, lending primacy to an attitude that aids the maintenance of a static, passionless equilibrium. Non-interference, fatalism, defeat: a refusal to break away from "religious theatre" in order to take a serious look at what is happening in the streets: this, says Naipaul, is an example of the writer abdicating his office. Narayan fiddles while India burns.

It is not necessary to number the dubious suppositions on which Naipaul bases his tenebrous account of India. Capable insiders such as Nissim Ezekiel have already furnished superb rejoinders to such books as *An Area of Darkness* and *A Wounded Civilization*, censuring the writer and his works on several fronts. Naipaul has been variously shown-up for his brazen streamlining of *karmic* philosophy (which, incidentally, cannot be separated from the dynamics of *dharma*), his attribution of epic causes to single events, his dizzy overviews derived from the eccentric and the particular, his orientalist yardsticks (social, ethical, literary), and his personal bloody-mindedness.

Today, however, my concern is not with Naipaul's views on India but rather the manner in which he views Narayan viewing India. And this is precisely the crux of the matter: Naipaul feels that Narayan's stories about India elide too much in rendering a seamless account of a world coming apart at the seams, while Narayan contends, as he must, that his stories are about caricatural Malgudians in an imaginary Malgudi. They do not, as such, even pretend to narrativise the shifting, colliding landscapes of reality, whether they are interior or exterior, psychic or empiric.

The argument may seem jejune, if not outrightly archaic, but it encapsulates the worldviews of two writers with vastly dissimilar legacies. Naipaul is a legatee of the post-Romantic tradition of psychological realism and considers the novel "a form of social inquiry" (18); his stance — whether fairly or unfairly — is that of an *engage* writer narrativising socio-political realities, assessing the ideological formations that govern the motives and actions of individuals, institutions, and communities. In this context, it would be unnatural for him to privilege aestheticism over verism. Narayan, on the other hand, is concerned primarily with imparting comic pleasure (*vasa*) at the expense of *le realisme*; the world he creates is a fantastic enclave inhabited by characters who reflect a caricatural reality that can never, no matter how fertile the human imagination, be taken as an approximation to phenomenal reality. He invents an aberrant microcosm in which complex realities are displaced so that even the verisimilar and the probable strike us as sensational transferences to the remote and the improbable. Naipaul, in this sense, commits a critical blunder by identifying Malgudi — notwithstanding his concession that the writer simplifies reality — with actual India. Once he makes the correspondence, then it becomes natural for him to express dissatisfaction with this insular milieu where privation and distress are under erasure.

The confusion, it seems, is in some measure generic, since Naipaul would have Narayan write comic novels which do not occlude the distressing actualities of India. According to his prescription, the comic must be subordinate to the critical, though this would entail subverting the genre of pure comedy and enfeebling its laughter-inducing properties. One suspects that Naipaul would prefer Narayan to write in the mode of *A House for Mr. Biswas*, where the comedy is dialogically presented while the plot is intensely tragic in conception. Narayan's agenda, however, is very different from Naipaul's. His principal aim is to stimulate aesthetic pleasure in risible situations and, as such, he addresses the consummate epicurean rather than the conscientious humanitarian. If this is a form of hedonistic abdication, then it arises from the writer's desire to work within the rigorous conventions of his chosen genre. It is, at best, unfair to indict a writer for excelling in his type of comedy simply because the genre, or more accurately the sub-genre, refuses to accommodate unpalatable realities and, when it does, domesticates them to fit a caricatural milieu. To pose the obvious question, then: What exactly is Narayan's type of comedy? And why does its successful deployment involve the prescribing of what Ortega Y Gasset called "lived realities" and that schematising of hieratic subjects? I should prefer to answer these questions with reference to *The Man-Eater of Malgudi*, but with the caution that my broad schema may not be applicable at all times to all his novels.

The *Man-Eater* posits a parodic simulation of some extant social actuality so that, even when we do identify elements which belie one or another diurnal circumstance, we recognise them as streamlined "patterns", or, to be more exact, animated silhouettes of that circumstance and not the circumstance itself. We are witness to a para-real, hermetically sealed world where the normal is stylised to the extent that we begin to wonder at the extraordinary in the ordinary. This serves a double purpose: it ratifies the view that Malgudi is not a fictive rendition of actual India, thus guarding us against any subjective engagement in the human drama while ensuring by this very fact our endorsement of the "other" rationale that inspires life in Malgudi. The story is, however, told in the first person, thereby obliging us to see everything through the dubious eyes of the narrating character. It can be argued that the simulated atmosphere of Malgudi results from Nataraj's, not Narayan's, extroverted perspective; this, however, would require us to explain why the same two-dimensional quality prevails in his other novels about Malgudi.

The *Man-Eater* falls under the rubric of *comedie de moeurs*, a genre that stipulates a restricted milieu with social codes and value-systems which, though generalised, are clearly delineated so that we derive a sense of a closely knit, autonomous universe. In this mode of comedy, human figures are employed to personify abstract concepts; embody humours, sentiments; illustrate habits, trends; and exemplify types, stereotypes. This method of flattening characters serves to undermine our subjective empathy, for we cannot identify their suffering as potentially human (something that occurs when we meet tragic individuals such as Hamlet and Lear), thus negating catharsis through pity and fear. Narayan's scale is ordinary from the very outset; there is never a hint that characters and events will transcend their mundane proportions, traverse the metaphysical scale of tragedy. The beginning itself is suitably banal. Nataraj describes his profession, his ablutionary routine, and his indolent friends, thereby setting the physical context (the printery) for the main comic encounter, limning the behavioural history of Malgudians (who contribute to the incidental and coincidental moments of levity) as well as introducing the central players (Nataraj, Sastri, Vasu) who actuate the structural progression from apparent order to apparent disorder and back to apparent order. But, more significantly, the narrative perspective from the very beginning establishes a "contrary" universe where serious actions are refracted and subverted rather than reflected and imitated. Malgudi is a collateral world that suggests a parodic likeness, thus an actual unlikeness, to an original world. It is, as it were, an idealised simulacrum of an untranslatable original. A recognition of this paradox of unlikeness in likeness, incongruity in congruity, fuels our sense of the ridiculous and induces a comic reaction.

Narayan achieves a comic response through realmic analogy that conceals a deeper contrast. Thus his text seems to be based on those "incongruity theories" of laughter identified by writers such as Beattie, Kant, Bergson, and Schopenhauer. As Schopenhauer says,

> The cause of laughter is in every case simply the sudden perception of the incongruity between a concept and the real objects to which it has been related in our mind....All laughter then is occasioned by a paradox, and therefore by unexpected assimilation, whether this is expressed in words or in actions. (355).

Narayan has, in his repertoire, a number of strategic devices that effect various forms of incongruity on the perceptual level, thus inspiring laughter. Some of these are role-reversals, aptronymic irony, caricature and disproportion, mock-heroism, comic paranoia and complaint, verbal hyerbole, optical bathos, mock-sanctity and mock-violation, and the inversion of ideas. Take, for example, the device of aptronymic irony implied by the names Vasu and Nataraj. *Vasu* stands for good, abundant, or wealthy; Vasus are a "class of gods regarded as atmospheric powers" (i.e., the Rudras, the Advityas, the Asvins, and the Maruts); they are invoked for several reasons, mainly to help "cure convulsions and other maladies; to prevent enemies interfering with sacred rites and ceremonies; to allay discord; and to bestow treasures on their worshippers" (Stutley 217). In comparing the Vedic Vasus with the Vasu of Malgudi, Narayan invites us to effect a mechanical conjunction that leads to a sudden perceptual disjunction as we unite the two versions — the sacred and the profane — in one complex instant of appreciation. The ludicrous assails us the moment we realise that Vasu, unlike his ethereal ancestors, petrifies instead of preserves Nature. Nataraj is similarly treated by Narayan. Shiva, the Lord of the Dance, the Unmoved Mover, whose activity denotes the eternal dynamic of creation, maintenance, and destruction, is in *The Man-Eater* an ineffectual and cowardly printer who cannot even meet the deadlines set by his clients, far less counter the threat posed by Vasu to his own and to Malgudi's equanimity. Here, again, we experience a sense of the ridiculous that is brought about by an insight into the real disjunction betrayed by the simulated conjunction.

In the limited scope of this essay, I cannot provide too many examples of the subjective and intellectual grounds on which a spectator may respond to comedy. It is, nevertheless, manifestly clear that comedy subsumes an aesthetic principle (i.e., the spectator's response to an objective situation) and a unifying structure (i.e., plot, theme, context) which creates an objective situation amenable to the comic impulse. In *The Man-Eater* the objective situation, as I have already shown, depends on a simple movement from harmony to disharmony and back to harmony. Narayan's type of comedy, however, can be properly understood only when we see how he plays with proportions (physical and conceptual) against the backdrop of his three-tiered structure.

Narayan's territory is not merely socially and geographically circumscribed, but its inhabitants are also limned as singular types, so that their experiential scale is vastly diminished. Sen and the poet, for instance, never range beyond their respective follies — politics and poetry — while Sastri (the wise one, the expositor of sastras) is capable only of grasping the world through religious allegory. Malgudi is a

diminutive world with diminutive characters whose *dharma* seems to
involve the endless deferral of tasks, inconclusive armchair discourses,
excursive "whinges" about everything from Nehru to aerated drinks,
and an attitude of inaction and lethargy whereby things are allowed to
take their course, regardless of their long-term implications. Malgudi,
then, is permeated with an air of quirky banality, a fizzy uniformity;
its denizens are not ruled by moral rigour nor ruined by great passions.
Their moments of intemperance, when not contrived, are harmlessly
evanescent, their verbal fencing routine and atmospheric rather than
abrasive and didactic. All in all, we have a world where things just
happen with the least amount of input on the part of its inhabitants.
Enter into this small-scale universe the large-scale Vasu: now the scene
is set for the encounter between Nataraj, who intends good but has poor
resources, and the *rakshas* Vasu, who intends evil and has the resources
to realise his aims.

Narayan, it is most evident, builds up a clash of proportions (physical,
emotional and conceptual) by unleashing an apparent colossus (with
the passion, ambition, prejudice and myopia to match his monstrous
bulk) on the somnolent midgets — so to speak — of Malgudi. But this
fact, I must hasten to add, should not lead to the misconception that
Vasu has the character traits of a complex individual. He is an individual,
as Nataraj is an individual, but only within the simulacral arena of
Malgudi. We, the readers, recognise him as the *a priori* type of the
choleric bully, the irascible *pehalwaan* who wreaks havoc in his ambition
to the source of all activity. Vasu is, in one sense, doomed from the
very start by the narrator's description of him; he is immediately
domesticated, reduced to caricature, but in a way that suggests his
violent misplacement in the town of Malgudi:

[The poet's} head suddenly vanished, and a moment later a new
head appeared in its place — a tanned face, large powerful eyes
under thick eyebrows, a large forehead and a shock of unkempt
hair like a black halo.

He came forward, practically tearing aside the curtain, an act
that violated the sacred traditions of my press. I said, "Why don't
you kindly take a seat in the next room? I'll be with you in a
moment." He paid no attention, but stepped forward, extending his
hand....He gave me a hard grip. My entire hand disappeared into
his fist — he was a huge man, about six feet tall. He looked quite

slim, but his bull-neck and hammer-fist revealed his true stature.
(15)

This mock-satanic account foreshadows Vasu's *adharmic* deeds,
but it also suggests that he is a towering colossus only from the lilliputian
perspective of the paranoiac exaggerator Nataraj, and only in the deflated
context of Malgudi. In the course of the story, Nataraj's fervid imagination
triggers off paranoiac asides and romantic excursions that raise our
doubts about his reliability. The creator is, we suspect, a slave to his
fancy.

It is rewarding to consider the passage on a more theoretical level.
In presenting Vasu as a dark angel, Narayan makes use of the classical
notion of physical ugliness as a measure of moral turpitude. Vasu
breaks the norms of civilised behaviour, no doubt, but he also commits
moral transgressions that are distasteful to the *ahimsaic* beliefs of the
deeply religious Malgudians. Into a passionless and *dharmic* society, he
brings passion and *adharma*, thus tilting the scales of moral equilibrium.
It is this unthinkable apostasy that initially attracts Nataraj to Vasu: the
man of inaction is captivated by the man of action; the timid conformist
is mesmerised by the arrogant maverick; the paterfamilias covets the
experience of the philanderer. Much of the humour in *The Man-Eater*
is generated by the exchanges between these two polar characters, one
invested with an excess of bad faith, the other sustained by a rickety
faith that obliges him to safeguard his *dharma*. Again we see how the
perception of an incongruity stokes our sense of the ridiculous; moreover,
Nataraj and Vasu, not to mention Sen and Sastri, are all unfinished
men; and as such, their actions and reactions are often predictable,
their behaviour sometimes machine-like— which justifies, to some
degree, Bergson's notion of laughter emanating from our perception
of the "mechanical encrusted on the living" (37).

It needs to be mentioned, however, that even as he composes his
comic stage through a series of little touches (e.g., the pitting together
of discrepant elements; verbal parries, repartees; the transposition of
characters, situations), Narayan organises his plot around the process
of *katastasis;* that is, the incitement of our concern and its subsequent
negation on the basis that there was no grounds for it in the first place.
It should be stated, at this juncture, that our concern assumes an
exalted form only when Kumar, the temple elephant, is endangered.
This is because we never truly identify with any of the characters, not

even Nataraj. We do *support* him as the guardian of *dharma,* but it is impossible for us to admire his personal qualities in the way that we admire the wit in a play by Wycherley or Etherege. In fact, our sympathy lies with the elephant — not as beast, but as symbol of order and *dharma.* There is, then, no clear line separating the wits from the butts in *The Man-Eater;* Malgudians oscillate between two poles, depending on their presence of mind, individual initiative, and territorial advantage. The structural unit and the spectator-response are, I have said, related in terms of a broader paradigm, where initial order (Malgudi before Vasu) is linked to the absence of spectator-concern; the extreme point of disorder (Vasu's nefarious designs on Kumar) is related to the arousal of spectator-concern; and the restitution of order (Vasu's failure through self-destruction) is tied up with the process of *katastasis:* the relaxation of spectator-concern achieved through the rejection of its causal grounds. This last movement pitches us headlong into the realm of the absurd.

Any discussion of *katastasis* in *The Man-Eater* presupposes a study of the mythic scheme that is superimposed on the mechanical plot and which affects the way it is conceptually resolved. The three-tiered structure of order-disorder-order has its Hindu parallel in *dharma-adharma-dharma.* Vasu, the *rakshas* embodying *himsa* (violence or injury), *anrta* (falsehood), *nikrti* (immorality) and *maya* (deceit), violates the *dharmic* world of Malgudi with his *tamasic* (dark, destructive) activity. This larger violation is foreshadowed very early in the novel by this violation of the inner sanctum of the printery, which is demarcated by a blue (the celestial hue) curtain. Vasu fits the (mock-) archetype of the *rakshas* who acquires immense powers through *tapasya* (ascetic practices) but whose *hubris* turns him against those very forces which have empowered him. His cruel treatment of his guru is a flagrant example; but, more notably, we see this in his conduct towards Nataraj. The non-paying tenant sets out to destroy the tolerant landlord. Vasu throws down the gauntlet when he breaks the sanctity of the blue curtain, and the scene is ready for the mock-war between Nataraj, the reluctant guardian of *dharma,* and Vasu, the willing agent of anarchy.

Narayan's mythic paradigm serves to anticipate the development and the conclusion of the story. We, in fact, rely on prior texts (and in particular the *Ramayana)* for the story's conceptual framework. So much so, that by the time we come to Sastri's prophetic reference to the Bhasmasura episode from the *Ramayana,* we already have an idea about Vasu's ultimate destiny. But it would be wrong to read the story as a moral fable reinforcing a worldview that is rigidly Hindu. Narayan achieves something more complicated by grafting a hieratic serious, sacred) text on a demotic (popular, profane) one. However, it is not the hieratic that modifies the demotic, but the other way round, inasmuch as levity undercuts gravity. In this context, the purely didactic exists in the hieractic text and has only a mock-presence in the demotic one. This is because Narayan's aim is aesthetic rather than ameliorative; we derive pleasure *(Vasa)* from the perception of a discrepancy between the ludicrous realm of *The Man-Eater* the sublime realm of the *Ramayana*. Vasu's self-annihilation is, for instance, comic because it is accidental and ironic: the man who would destroy the largest mammal on earth is overcome by an insignificant mosquito. The hieratic episode to which we are referred is Bhasmasura's destruction by his own hand as narrated in the *Ramayana,* though, unlike Narayan's comic representation, Valmiki's original version is epical, if not quasi-tragic, for Bhasmasura is out-manoeuvred by no less than Lord Vishnu. Order, it is crucial to note, is restored in Malgudi only after we learn of the circumstances surrounding Vasu's death—and not before it. This is partly because the narrator is implicated in the affair, but mainly because murder has no place in idyllic Malgudi. After the nature of Vasu's death is conveyed to Nataraj by the glib Sastri, we revert to a pre-Vasuan, and not a modified post-Vasuan, world of *dharma*. The *rakshas* was merely an aberration, neither adding to nor substracting from the theatre of Malgudi.

And so reassured, we are suspended in that other text, and the quarrels in our middle earth (which is caught between "once upon a time" and "happily ever after") have ceased to exist. At least for the textual moment.

Note

1.   See Nissim Ezekiel, "Naipaul's India and Mine." *New Writing in India.* Ed. Adil Jussawalla. Harmondsworth" Penguin, 1974. 70-90.

Works Cited

Bergson, Henri. *Laughter: An Essay on the Meaning of the Comic.* Trans, C. Brereton and F. Rothwell. London: Macmillan, 1911.

Naipaul, V.S. India: *A Wounded Civilization.* Harmondsworth: Penguin, 1979.

Narayan, R.K. *The Man-Eater of Malgudi.* Harmondsworth: Penguin, 1983.

Schopenhauer, Arthur. "The World as Will and Idea." *Theories of Comedy.* Ed. P. Lauter. New York: Anchor, 1964.

Stutley, James and Margaret, eds. *A Dictionary of Hinduism.* Bombay: Allied, 1977.

10

THE POWER OF WOMEN IN R. K. NARAYAN'S NOVELS

BRITTA OLINDER
(University of Gothenburg)

Almost all academics nowadays are aware of Michel Foucault's view that power is everywhere. Yes, power is indeed ubiquitous; it is a complex, often elusive concept that can be defined and used in many ways. There are different types of public power, such as political or economic power; not least, in the Indian context, we may think of the power of multinational companies. In Sweden a state commission of highly qualified people have been working for some five years investigating where real power in the country is wielded, whether by politicians or administrators or by big businessmen — or somebody else. This is often difficult to sort out, because in both the public and the private spheres there is real power and formal power. There is also a mixture of the public and private in the lives of ordinary people who are exposed to the power of administrators, of teachers (as their pupils), or of doctors (as their patients). It is generally agreed that power is not a static quality but has to do with the relationship between people; a form of energy; the capacity to make somebody else do what they would not do otherwise. In the private sphere, many kinds and degrees of power may thus be summed up in power over one's own life and power over somebody else's. The balancing of these two can be seen as the basic problem of close relationships such as those between husband and wife. In this context, we might also note that lack of power has been the object of much recent research into marginalised groups. Feminist scholarship may be seen as a study of powerlessness.[1]

In trying to define R.K. Narayan's presentation of female characters, I have found it interesting to classify them in terms of their relations of power to men and to explore the reasons for those relations. They fall into three main groups: first, dominating, powerful women; second, powerless, frustrated, oppressed women; and third, women accepting the system — in this case, the Indian society of strong masculine dominance — but at the same time finding ways and means to informal, indirect control of their situation. The aim would be to see if any of them have any real power and, if so, of what kind.

In the first category of dominating women we may distinguish between the tyranny of termagants and the influence of those women who, through their attractiveness and capacity for fascinating men and evoking their love, gain power over them. Most of the time the women whom Narayan calls termagants appear in passing, in very subordinate roles, such as Gangu in *The Dark Room*. She is Savitri's, the main character's, friend. Her eccentricity is described in these terms: "She left home when she pleased and went where she liked, moved about without an escort, stared back at people and talked loudly. Her husband never interfered with her but let her go her own way, and believed himself to be a champion of women's freedom" (16). In the same novel Ponni, the tinker's wife, is another example of dominating women. Here we get the mixture of the shrew and the woman who attracts love, because Mari, her husband, is a burglar: "to please his wife. He was intensely devoted to her, and her one ambition in life was to fill a small brass pot with coins and precious metal"; and since a tinker's labours tend to yield an inadequate income, it will make a "a wife unhappy and quarrelsome. Mari cared a great deal for his wife, although he chased her about and threw things at her when he was drunk" (81). Ponni, however, knows how to manage him. She says:

> He is a splendid boy, but sometimes he goes out with bad friends, who force him to drink, and then he will come home and try to break all the pots and beat me. But when I know that he has been drinking, the moment he comes home, I trip him up from behind and push him down, and sit on his back a little while; he will wriggle a little, swear at me and then sleep, and wake up in the morning quiet as a lamb. I can't believe any husband is unmanageable in this universe" (90). This is the comic opposite of the experience of Savitri, with the more educated woman's handicap. Other women who have the power of attracting a man and, at least in

certain situations, making him do whatever they want, are Shanta
Bai, also in *The Dark Room,* Bharati in *Waiting for the Mahatma,*
Rosie in *The Guide,* and Daisy in *The Painter of Signs.*

The complex play of power between Raju and Rosie in *The Guide*
begins with his falling in love with her, which means that she has a
hold on him. Later, he can help her, and she needs his company in
her loneliness — something that gives him some control. Then,
increasingly, he neglects his own affairs, because the only reality of his
life and consciousness in Rosie: "All my mental powers were now
turned to keep her within my reach, and keep her smiling all the time,
neither of which was at all easy" (118). This shows, in retrospect, that
he is under her spell, in her power. However, when she is left by her
husband on the railway platform and comes to Raju's house, we see the
display of mutual power shifting from one to the other: his hold on her
as he encourages and supports her, hers in her attraction for him. In
this situation he can say: "My guidance was enough. She accepted it
in absolutely unquestioning faith and ignored everything else completely.
It gave me a tremendous confidence in myself and seemed to enhance
my own dimensions" (167). He organises engagements for her as a
dancer and supports her in turning her talent into a public success.
Now he thinks in terms of explicit power: "I had a monopoly of her
and nobody had anything to do with her....She was my property" (189).
That is why he keeps others away from her when she has become
famous as a dancer. He does work as her manager, helping her to the
power or satisfaction of exercising her art as well as of receiving public
acclaim; but he has also taken for himself the power of exploiting the
situation in his own favour. His lack of power in this context is shown
when he tries to mix with her artist friends and when he is feeling like
an interloper as he tries to make them leave. It is really a mere show
of power without real substance. For fear of losing what authority he
has, his exploitation of her becomes criminal. He is arrested and then
let out on bail — paid by her. Now he becomes a "hanger-on in the
house; ever since she had released me from police custody, the mastery
had passed to her" (218). He feels his powerlessness more and more
as he is condemned to prison for his forgery of her name while she,
after all, continues her every-more-successful career, now without his
help.

If we go to the other novels, we find that the relations between
Sriram and Bharati in *Waiting for the Mahatma* and Raman and Daisy

in *The Painter of Signs* show many parallels. In both cases the woman is politically conscious and working for a cause, demanding her admirer to join her in those endeavours. In both cases the young man is weaker and cannot fully engage himself in this task. His first aim is, all the time, the woman he is in love with.

At first Sriram finds Bharati "A very ill-tempered and sharp-tongued girl" (48), " a termagant" (51). He compares her to the woman who has brought him up, who has the authority of both father and mother: "You have the same style of talk as my grandmother. She is as sharp-tongued as you are" (51). We may note that he is conditioned by his grandmother to obey a woman. Very soon we see him pleading with Bharati to let him work for the same cause with her: "Why don't you take me as your pupil?" (53) he asks. He can ask her pathetically why she is angry with him. Of course, we have to see the power game intertwined with all the usual feelings and reactions of somebody falling in love, of wishing to be close to the loved one, etc. Here there are also, however (for the sake of his beloved), all the demands on him for dedication to a cause, the cause of Indian independence—something that will, in fact, keep him far from her. So, for his love, he has to change, to learn to spin like a true Gandhi disciple, to serve his country, to live a life in utter simplicity, even be prepared to die. Bharati is shown to encourage him, which implies a position of indirect power; she looks after him; she is his guru, the one who teaches him to spin, and she proves herself to be a taskmistress of no mean order. She also expects Sriram to be afraid of her because she is his guru. His reaction, in the Indian tradition of male-female relations, is: "The whole thing is extremely false. She ought to be my wife and come to my arms" (93). But he finds himself in an unorthodox power relation: "Absurd that a comely young woman should be set to educate a man" (93-94).

While Bharati's cause is Gandhi's cause, comprehensive and idealistic, Daisy's in *The Painter of Signs* is more specifically social, focussing on family planning. She, too, however, would love to behave like a guru for such a disciple, Raman thinks. At a later stage he declares himself her slave, something she thinks he should feel ashamed of. At one point, "He was resolved not to be submissive and timid, but prove himself her equal in toughness. She should learn to respect him and not treat him as if he were a hanger-on to be spoken to when it pleased her or dropped at other times" (98). This is after the incident when

Raman has tried to rape Daisy in the dark — demonstrating his male physical strength — while she has slipped away, using her feminine wiles.

Daisy, the modern liberated women, explicitly talks about this conscious need to keep all the power over her own life: "If you want to marry me, you must leave me to my own plans even after I am a wife. On any day you question why or how, I will leave you" (159). What disturbs him later, when they are planning to live as man and wife, is "her habit of separating 'his' from 'hers' and her lack of interest in any joint venture" (167). He, on the other hand, is prepared to renounce the usual power of a husband and realises, for instance, that "the path of peace lay in not contradicting her" (168). When finally she leaves him for good, his sadness is mixed with relief and "great satisfaction of having his own way at last" (183).

When we come to oppressed women, the most comprehensive picture is that of Savitri, in *The Dark Room*. What is interesting here is her growing awareness of her own powerlessness. Already in the first chapter her reactions to her husband's total insensitivity to her feelings and her dignity in relation to their children and revealing: "How impotent she was, she thought; she had not the slightest power to do anything at home, and after fifteen years of married life... she felt that she ought to have asserted herself a little more at the beginning of her married life" (8). Later on in the novel she tries, however, to assert her own rights: "I'm a human being.... You men will never grant that. For you we are playthings when you feel like hugging, and slaves at other times. Don't think you can fondle us when you like and kick us when you choose" (88). But then she realises the weakne of her position: "'I don't possess anything in this world. What possessions can a woman call her own except her body? Everything else that she has is her father's, her husband's, or her son's'" (75). And when Ramani claims that the children are his only: "Yes, you are right. They are yours, absolutely. You paid the midwife and the nurse. You pay for their clothes and teachers. You are right. Didn't I say that a woman owns nothing?'" (76).

We may notice in this context that Ramani, often a victim of self-deception, may assume a tone of authority and treat Savitri as a child: "You have a lot to learn yet. You are still a child, perhaps a precocious child, but a child all the same" (14). At the same time, he is very proud of his wife: "He surveyed her slyly, with a sense of satisfaction at possessing her. When people in the theatre threw looks at her, it increased his satisfaction all the more.... He enjoyed his role of husband so much that he showed her a lot of courtesy" (21). It is the same man who becomes infatuated with the independent, professional woman Shanta Bai, who (by showing her lack of concern) draws him increasingly into her net. This makes him even more insensitive to his wife than before and thus triggers off the tragedy. As a background, we should also keep in mind the pattern and ideal of a wife in Indian myth, the perfectly loving and self-sacrificing, goddesslike Savitri. Narayan's use of the same name for his anti-heroine gives the story new dimensions.

When we come to women accepting the traditional system, we can point, first, to Savitri's reliable friend in *The Dark Room* called Janamma, who "never moved very freely among people" (17) and would have to be at home when her husband was expected. She maintains that wives have to be good and patient, whatever their husbands are doing, and gives Savitri some examples: "her own grandmother who slaved cheerfully for her husband who had three concubines at home; her aunt who was beaten every day by her husband and had never uttered a word of protest for fifty years; another friend of her mother's who was prepared to jump into a well if her husband so directed her" (42). This is the traditional pattern of a good Indian wife in total subjection to her husband and master. Here we might also refer to Rosie's powerlessness in her role as Marco's wife in *The Guide,* and her difficulty in wishing to uphold tradition and yet protesting against its restrictions.

In Nagaraj's wife, Sita, of *The World of Nagaraj,* we can study the traditional woman who accepts her subjection but, because of her personality, has great natural authority. She is slaving for her husband and his family, and Nagaraj recognises that she "has not had a day's rest, serving me and my mother ungrudgingly" (5); she has "become a prisoner in the home" (14), something that would indicate powerlessness. However, this very fact has made him, Nagaraj, "a prisoner of domesticity," which would really imply his lack of power. This may also be illustrated by his frequently having to refrain from saying things: "Have to be careful and diplomatic all the time, the tightrope-walking called domestic harmony (4).

Sita is described as confined to her house and the temple, but she is, in fact, a source of strength and good judgement, deeply admired by

Nagaraj, who many times (when he has not followed her advice), has to recognise that she was right: "His wife had a genius for doing the right thing, and he felt a profound gratitude for her attention" (9). There are, of course, also many other occasions when she does not understand him, and we can see the comedy of misunderstanding develop between them. His recognition of her, however, comes back like a refrain: "She has uncanny forethought.... I should hereafter leave everything to her — all management and decisions" (40). When they are having problems with Nagaraj's nephew and find it difficult to get to talk to him, Nagaraj dramatises the situation to the point of seeing Sita in terms of Lady Macbeth, handing him the dagger and egging him on (66). He feels that she is commanding him; unrelenting, she orders him peremptorily; he has to appease her — all of which seems to indicate that he feels her power to make him do what he does not want. Occasionally we can find Sita fuming inside at her husband's way of speaking, thus observing wifely manners while at the same time reacting very strongly against her husband. Sometimes, however, he is nagged by her or cowed just by her appearance. We will also see her commanding her husband "to leave for the village, otherwise she threatened to go herself" (155). Nagaraj then comments: "What are women coming to these days, ordering men about?" However, he generally feels that Sita has much better capacity to deal with human problems. We may, thus, ask about this traditional Indian relationship: Who has the power? It is revealing when, in a reversed feminist formula, Nagaraj asserts triumphantly that, like a married woman who does not want to be described only as her husband's wife, "He had established his standing not as one married to Sita" but as somebody who will have achieved something on his own: He looks forward to the completion of the book on Narada, which he has set as his goal in life (181).

One comment on all the examples mentioned here is that none of the women initiate a love relationship. They feel, or try to feel, affection for their husbands; they perform the duties of love, but they are not seen to fall in love. That is a male prerogative in Narayan — and even so, unorthodox. In traditional Indian society, marriages are arranged by the families, and Western romantic love as a way of choosing a partner is considered unwise; hence, the authority of parents in a relationship between man and woman is here another aspect of the power complex.

The statements at the beginning of this paper, on power being everywhere around us, are thus confirmed as far as relations between men and women in Narayan's novels are considered. How elusive power often is, how fluctuating it is and how many times it is difficult to locate exactly have also been illustrated. Again, I wish to refer to the ambiguities of formal and real power, since in this area the husband has all formal power in traditic ial Indian society. In Narayan's case, we should not forget the decisive influence of patterns from Hindu myths. The role of the original Savitri is a case in point as well as an example of what we may call the power of the powerless. This, in turn, can be related to the idea of non-violence, the power of those who consciously renounce power, as in Gandhi's teaching. Related to this is what emerged about love, making the person succumbing to that emotion powerless, while conveying power to the person loved.

Power is a concept that can, of course, also be tried out in other relationships than that between man and woman. Narayan has interesting examples of the power game between the strong and the weak man, where tables are often turned in the end, as well as cases of a son's power over his father.

Another aspect again is the way in which power is mostly felt to lie outside you, with other people. What would the story of Nagaraj be from his wife's point of view or *The Dark Room* from the husband, Ramani's? I think we would see that if power is everywhere, powerlessness is felt to be even much more so.

Notes

1. Of the many works in this area, I have found the following to be particularly helpful: Nancy C.M. Hartsock, *Money, Sex, and Power: Toward a Feminist Historical Materialism* (London: Longman, 1984); Yvonne Hirdman, *Om Makt: Maktutredningen, Rapport 5 (On Power: State Commission on Power, Report 5* (Uppsala, 1986; and David A. Baldwin, *Paradoxes of Power* (Oxford: Blackwell, 1989).

2. See Narayan's version in *Gods, Demons, and Others* (London: Heinemann, 1965) 182-189.

Works Cited

Narayan, R.K. *The Dark Room*. New Delhi: Orient, 1976.

—, *The Guide*. London: Bodley, 1970.

—, *The Painter of Signs*. London: Heinemann, 1977.

—, *Waiting for the Mahatma*. East Lansing: Michigan State UP, 1955.

—, *The World of Nagaraj*. Mysore: Indian Thought, 1990.

11

MAHATMA GANDHI IN R.K. NARAYAN AND CHAMAN NAHAL

K. RADHA
(University of Kerala)

Mahatma Gandhi, who believed that novels were generally about love and that they told lies and made people gullible with fine words, became, ironically enough, an important figure in Indian fiction in English. His impact on Indians is so profound that he appears as a character in a large number of novels and short stories; in many others, he is behind the scene, and his influence is felt by the characters. For more than three decades, till his death in 1948, he was responsible for several far-reaching changes in the social, political, and economic spheres of his nation. These epoch-making developments led to the treatment of hitherto neglected themes such as the problems of the harijans (untouchables), the downtrodden, and the oppressed in a serious manner by Indian-English writers.

One of the earliest novels showing Gandhi's influence is K.S. Venkataramani's *Murugan the Tiller* (1927); it becomes stronger in his later novel *Kandan the Patriot* (1932). K. Nagarajan's Galsworthian family chronicle *Athavar House* (1937), his *Chronicles of Kedaram* (Gandhi appears to mediate in one of the feuds in the small town), and above all Mulk Raj Anand's *Untouchable* (1935) and Raja Rao's *Kanthapura* (1938) are some of the early novels written under the spell cast by the Mahatma. The followers of the great national leader appear also in later novels, such as Narayan's *The Vendor of Sweets*, and Nayantara Sahgal's *A Time to be Happy*, while in *Motherland* (1944), by C.N. Zutshi, we get caricatures of Gandhi, Nehru and others (Gandhi is portrayed as Lord Krishna, piping to the people on his spiritual flute, and his followers flock around him like the *gopis* of yore, dancing to his tunes).   Venu Chitale's *In Transit* (1950) deals with Gandhi's magnetic personality; Raj Gill's *The Rape* (1958) blames Gandhi for all the bloodshed and rapes after partition, although the novel ends on a different note; and Manohar Malgonkar, in *A Bend in the Ganges* (1964), also holds Gandhi responsible for what happened after Partition, as does Chaman Nahal in his novel *Azadi* (1975).   Gandhi is a major figure in Nahal's *The Crown and the Loincloth* (1981) and *The Salt of Life* (1990) also.

Gandhi, with his patriotism, his love of truth, and his practice of non-violence, became a true Indian hero, and for several decades he was worshipped like a god.   This made him a myth, a *mahatma*, a man with a great soul.   He saw no dichotomy between religion and politics; he wanted Indians to act, and he "animated, revitalised, and re-enacted all the symbolic dramas of the *Mahabharatha* as no intellectual 'Pandit' ever could," as Amaury de Reincourt phrased it in *The Soul of India* (315).   Gandhi was transformed into a saviour figure.   According to the *Bhagavad Gita*, wherever there is a decline of goodness, God is born as man to punish the uprighteous and to protect the righteous (IV:7). Likewise, people thought that Gandhi's birth was the need of the hour.

Narayan's *Waiting for the Mahatma* (1955) was published seven years after the assassination of Gandhi.   [The title reminds us of Clifford Odets's *Waiting for Lefty* (1935) and Samuel Beckett's *Waiting for Godot* (1954).   It may be the hero's waiting for the Mahatma or the assassin's waiting for his prey.] The Mahatma himself appears in this novel and ironic comments on the reception of the Gandhian ideology are interspersed throughout.

The young hero Sriram's encounter with Gandhism begins at a vast public meeting held at Malgudi in the hot sun.   "Waiting for the Mahatma makes one very thirsty," thinks Sriram, who has to wait for Gandhi on the sands of the Sarayu (15).   Gandhi's very first appearance in the novel reveals the following qualities of his: his dislike for English, "The language of our rulers" (16); his awareness of certain good points and defects in every man; his love of the poor and backward classes; and his hatred of pomp.   Gandhi surprises everyone by going to a scavenger's house; not only that, he makes the chairman of the municipality accompany him.   Gandhi is amused when throughout the night the municipal chairman and other employees clean the surroundings. Sriram, who falls in love with Bharati, one of the followers of Gandhi, at first sight, is bent upon becoming Gandhi's follower in order to court Bharati and win her. The girl tells him curtly, "Anybody cannot be a volunteer" (35). However, the fact that Sriram is a motherless boy moves her. Sriram's grandmother does not like Gandhi: "For her the Mahatma was one who preached dangerously, who tried to bring untouchables into the temples and who involved people in difficulties with the police (41)." But Sriram becomes his follower when Gandhi receives him on Bharati's recommendation. Various phases of the freedom struggle in Gandhi's life are linked with the story of Sriram and Bharati. There is the Quit India Movement, Gandhi's arrests, the Swadeshi movement, the destruction of foreign goods, the Dandi March, India's getting independence, the partition, its aftermath, and finally the assassination of the Father of India. The Mahatma, before leaving for the prayer meeting at which he is shot dead, promises to conduct the marriage ceremony of Sriram and Bharati the following morning; he will be the priest and also act as the bride's father, he says.

The novel was not as favourably received as most of Narayan's other novels for, as Uma Parmeswaran points out, he does not use the devices that are his forte, "ambiguity, unsentimentality, humour and a lightness of spirit" (74). Further, Parameswaran says, "It is a Gandhian novel. Technically, Sriram is the hero of the novel and the plot revolves around him; but the predominant figure, even though he is seldom on stage, is Gandhi and the theme is Gandhism" (65).

She is highly prejudiced against this novel, for she considers it a failure: the portrait of Gandhi is weak and uninspiring, it lacks in "characterisation, and language" (65). Narayan, she writes, is "uninteresting when moulding good men, and positively out of his depth with supermen;" thus the novel fails because "Mahatma Gandhi was a superman. Sriram, the hero, is a good man" (66). Sriram is moronic, she adds, and Gandhi is in the same mould as a moron. Narayan takes certain familiar characteristics and incidents associated with Gandhi and he sticks them in haphazardly at the first opening he gets, adds Parameswaran, who also gives examples of Gandhi's speeches that are not well planned by the novelist. Narayan "merely drops Gandhi's statements like bricks" (67); thus, according to her, the characterisation of Gandhi is ineffective.

An American novelist friend of Narayan told him, "I think the book is weak in motivation; we don't learn anything about Mahatma Gandhi, and the narrative lacks punch" (qtd. in Narasimhaiah, *Swan* 155). And in *The Writer's Gandhi,* C.D. Narasimhaiah has observed that Narayan made a muddle of the Gandhian principle; he even suggests that he should withdraw the novel, complaining that the book does not enlarge our awareness of Gandhi or his era one bit. The novel, therefore, seems to him "pointless"; he is of the view that *Kanthapura* and Anand's *Untouchable* are incomparably superior "Gandhi-novels." A.N. Kaul feels that Gandhism as a political idea has meant little or nothing to Narayan. Very few critics are like William Walsh and consider the book a triumph, although P.S. Sundaram states that it is absurd to say that Narayan has not quickened our awareness of Gandhi in all his greatness.

Perhaps more than the hero, Sriram, and the heroine, Bharati, it is the minor characters (like the shopkeeper, Kanni, Sriram's grandmother, and Jagadish) who appeal to the reader. It is doubtful whether Sriram, whom Srinivasa Iyengar humorously describes as Malgudi's Bassanio, would have become Gandhi's follower if it were not for the Malgudi Portia, Bharati. Sriram, waiting for Bharati, has to wait for the Mahatma. M.K. Naik's comment that "Sriram's sudden conversion into a freedom fighter is unconvincing, because he is so obviously interested in Bharathi and not in *Bharat-mata* (Mother India)" (164) is quite apt, though to say that Narayan is not on sure ground, whether the scene is in Malgudi or Delhi is contestable. The book is neither a failure nor a triumph.

Nahal's *The Crown and the Loincloth* has for its background the turbulent times between 1915 and 1922. *[The Salt of Life* (1990) is its sequel].* The Crown and the Loincloth* opens with Gandhi sailing to India from abroad. He is seen aboard the *S.S. Arabia* "tossing in his bed" (19), musing on his sexual experiment. He is portrayed as a human being and not as a demi-god: "He was short. He was frail. And he was perhaps the ugliest man alive" (32). Like the storm outside, there is a storm in his mind, too.

All the major events of his past life flash upon his inward eye. He knows that there have been many denials. "He had quit sleeping with Kasturbai....He wouldn't eat on certain days. Were any of these a denial?" (15). Gandhi was always in the habit of questioning himself for every action of his, and this is very well brought out by Nahal.

Gandhi imagines certain people whom he knew rising with the angry waves. These accuse him of having punished them for what he had considered their moral lapses. Among these, his elder brother and his son, Harital, are also seen. He tries to justify his actions; he is happy that Kallenbach, who had vast properties in South Africa, had finally become a follower.

Gandhi, who was educated in England and imitated the English in dress and food, later undergoes a complete change. He knows,

> He was born a slave — in a slave nation. And wherever he went, the stigma of his birth went with him. He was an Indian, an *Indian*. A spineless fellow belonging to a spineless nation. A nation that was won by the sword of the mighty Englishmen and was being held by the sword. A nation utterly lacking in discipline. A nation of coolies, shoe-shine boys, and punkha-pullers. (2)

But Gandhi is sure that he is not spineless: "They may beat the life out of him, but they couldn't bend him. He would actually touch the feet of the lowliest, as before God they were all equal". (27)

> Gandhi's attitude to the Muslims is also one of tolerance: A Hindu may perhaps be happy to get rid of the Muslims, but he would be a stupid Hindu, an ignorant Hindu. For what would India be without the Muslims! Talk not to me of the atrocities they committed upon the Hindus and the Sikhs. Given the chance, the Hindus would have committed as many atrocities upon them. Talk to me instead of the beauty they have brought to India, talk to me of their architecture, of the roads they laid .... Bereft of the Muslims, India would be like a face with an eye missing. No, what touched the Muslims *should* touch the Hindus. The British were the common oppressors of them both. (129).

Gandhi, in real life, showed great shrewdness in judging people; and this aspect of his character is revealed in the scene in which Gandhi and the hero of the novel, Sunil, meet. Gandhi knows that many people want to join his ashram for easy food or to escape from domestic squabbles — some for self-importance. Nahal throws light on this trait of his character through a couple of apt comparisons: "They did not know Gandhi, though what a sifter of human beings he was. He had the jeweller's instinct for the precious stone or the wine taster's nose for the rich vintage" (132).

Another feature of Gandhi's character (namely, his sense of humour) is also not forgotten by the novelist; for example, when Motilal Nehru wants his son to take a little more time before he gets seriously involved in politics, Gandhi tells Motilal, "In England when the parents want to part lovers, they ask them to wait for a year" (324).

The various activities of Gandhi are mentioned briefly in the novel. In July 1920, Tilak passes away and Gandhi is in undisputed command. The same year the non-cooperation movement is advocated by Gandhi: "The British had destroyed the local industry" (130). In *Young India* and *Navajivan*, Gandhi lashed out at the government week after week, but when the police station at Chauri Chaura is burnt down, Gandhi calls off the non-cooperation movement, saying "we are not yet ready for non-violence, non-cooperation" (331). Motilal Nehru thinks that the "old man has gone insane" (331), and for some days Gandhi is so desperate that he even tells his wife that he could kill himself; but on her advice he goes on a fast for five days. While everyone blames Gandhi for giving up the movement, Nahal says, "Only one person in the entire nation believed Gandhi. Gandhi himself" (339). Gandhi has to bear the brunt of criticism for a long time, but when he is "not adored and adulated," and when he is spat upon, he can think more clearly than at other times.

After he is ruthlessly attacked at the AICC meeting in Delhi for suspending the non-cooperation movement, in the course of his walk he reaches the Yamuna near the bridge that connects Delhi with the trans-Yamuna area. It is a huge steel structure constructed by the British, but at once he thinks that the Indians are not ignorant of the art: there are bridges in Delhi that are four hundred years old. He is reminded of the splendid old forts and palaces in India built without the help of the British: "their stay here has been purely functional, devoid of beauty" (369); but the next moment he thinks along different lines and fluctuates between approval and accusation of the British.

Nahal tries to observe complete detachment and never ventures to pronounce a definite opinion either on the British or Gandhi, even though he is very sympathetic to Gandhi when he is in a state of mental unrest. We are made to see Gandhi mainly as he is seen by the British and by the Indians. General Dyer, who is a typical diehard Blimp, hates Gandhi: "The concessions the Government has made to that seditious Gandhi, the arch villain!" (85). Dyer thinks that he is causing nothing but trouble, and he is trying to placate the Muslims and carry them with him through sheer fraud. According to Dyer, Gandhi is crooked and scheming: "He lived in Ahmedabad, but showed up instantly where trouble was brewing. In Champaran. In Kheda. In Madras. In Bombay. Dyer often wondered if he had doubles to act for him" (186). He also *fanned* the trouble. Dyer's charges against Gandhi make a long list: "Made himself the self-appointed custodian of the affair, whether anyone wanted him to take the lead or not"; very cleverly he "made use of C.F. Andrews, this Reverend or that" (85); "To the Muslims he quoted the *Quran*, to these whites he must be quoting the *Bible*. And since the day the Rowlatt Acts had been gazetted, on March 18, 1919, he had thought of a new drama; a nation-wide *hartal*, a nation-wide strike" (86). Dyer condemns Gandhi's policy of non-violence as humbug, his multi-religious prayer meetings and community living as farce; he is in Jallianwalla Bagh to suppress the rebellion, but he is sad that the government has turned Gandhi back and does not allow him to proceed to the Punjab, "to lead these hooligans [Indians]," for Dyer would have "finished him with his own hands" (86). Kenneth Ashby, who is quite unlike Dyer and who is a sensible Indian Army Officer (he is a creation of Nahal), has fallen in love with Indians; but even he has no high opinion of Gandhi and calls him "a seditious rogue!"

In Nahal's novel the story of Gandhi (between 1915 and 1922) and the story of the people of Thakur Shanti Nath are very skilfully interwoven. Thakur Shanti Nath, a rich landowner, lives in Ajitha, which is Nahal's Kanthapura. While Shanti Nath is all the time loyal to the Crown, his son Sunil becomes a follower of the half-naked fakir in a loincloth. Professor K.R. Srinivasa Iyengar says that Nahal makes a rough sort of "Gandhi-Sunil equation." Sunil is as ordinary as Gandhi, and to a great extent resembles Moorthy in Raja Rao's *Kanthapura*. But our admiration for Sunil flags when he becomes a passionate lover of the married Muslim woman Rehana, who is a little older than he, and also another woman, Priti, of the hill tribe at Rohru, who is the wife to three brothers. Sunil is already married to Kusum and has a son; however, he dies a heroic death, typically Gandhian, while trying to save the Prince of Wales from terrorists.

The widow of Sunil, also a follower of Gandhi, goes to his Sabarmati ashram with her son Vikram. At the end of the novel, we see the Mahatma being arrested and taken to the jail on charges of sedition.

All that he carries with him are a couple of loincloths and some reading material like the *Gita,* the *Ramayana,* the *Quran,* the *Bible* and the ashram hymn book. He is sentenced to six years' imprisonment. The novel ends on a solemn note.

Gandhi, in Narayan's novel, does not impress the reader in spite of his direct appearances. In *The Crown and the Loincloth,* the novelist succeeds in weaving the story of Gandhi and that of Sunil and his family, giving equal importance to both. They merge quite naturally, without being yoked together by violence. Yet of the Gandhian protagonists, Sunil is the most morally unsound character, for he is willing to commit adultery. His tendency to have adulterous relations with women is a serious blemish on his character. Gandhi, too, refers to temptations in his life; but as he tells us in his autobiography, he was able to overcome them. He had a strong spirit, though the flesh was willing.

Nahal's portrait of Gandhi is more realistic and life-like than Narayan's: there is no idealisation or emulsification of Gandhi. The concluding sentence of the novel is superb: "For the time being, the lion in the loincloth was caged" (422). The Mahatma, whom Churchill described as a half-naked fakir, appears to have more flesh and blood in *The Crown and the Loincloth* than in *Waiting for the Mahatma.*

Works Cited

Nahal, Chaman. *The Crown and the Loincloth.* New Delhi: Vikas, 1981.

Naik, M.K. *A History of Indian English Literature.* New Delhi: Akademi, 1982.

Narasimhaiah, C.D. *The Swan and the Eagle: Essays on Indian English Literature.* Simla: Indian Institute, 1968.

—, *The Writer's Gandhi.* Patiala: Punjabi UP, 1967.

Parameswaran, Uma. *A Study of Representative Indo-English Novelists.* New Delhi: Vikas, 1976.

Reincourt, Amaury de. *The Soul of India.* London: Cape, 1961.

Srinivasa Iyengar, K.R. *Indian Writing in English.* New Delhi: Sterling, 1985.

12

R. K. NARAYAN'S BORDERLINE PEOPLE

R. RAMACHANDRA
(University of Mysore)

A significant feature of Narayan's world is that it is densely populated by borderline people: sanyasis, sorcerers, recluses, criminals, and the like. In fact, Narayan's creativity expresses itself, to a great extent, through a fascination with people who are at the borders of social life.

The Captain in *A Tiger for Malgudi*, who owns the Grand Malgudi Circus; Marco, in *The Guide,* who "dressed like a permanent tourist" and has "the appearance of a space traveller"; Rosie, also in *The Guide,* who is a devadasi; the shikari Alphonse in *The Man-Eater of Malgudi;* and Dr. Pal, in *The Financial Expert,* self-described as a sociologist, psychologist, journalist, author, and tourist director (as well as author of the semi-pornographic *Domestic Harmony),* are just a few of the numerous marginal people who inhabit Narayan's world —which is, in many respects, a microcosm of all Indian cities and villages.

These marginal, or liminal, people include those who lack the normal (or complete) social identities and who appear at the fringes of the social order. Dr. Pal, for example, does not establish his academic credentials at all and suggests the seamy side of Indian academic life, he ekes out his existence by participating in illegal or shady enterprises, he is, in essence, a social parasite. Others of his type are the Sanyasi who plucks flowers in the early mornings (in *The Bachelor of Arts*), the many children who populate *Swami and Friends*, and even the Spirit of Susila (in *The English Teacher*) with which Krishna communicates. The Inspector of Forms and Stationery in V.S. Naipaul's *An Area of Darkness*, which is a travel-commentary rather than a work of fiction, is yet another denizen of this world of marginal, liminal individuals.

A priest exists well within the Hindu social system, but the priest in *The Financial Expert,* who gives Margayya the mantra that will make him rich, calls himself a sanyasi; and a sanyasi, strictly speaking, stands completely outside the social system. Perhaps this fascination for the sanyasi will partly explain the conspicuous absence of caste in R.K. Narayan's works. The concept of *sanyas*—because it recognises the equality of not just all human beings but all living creatures— is inimical to a rigid caste system. The sanyasi in *A Tiger for Malgudi*, who calmly walks around with a tiger, reassures a frightened crowd: "You need not fear; he has only the appearance of a tiger...inside he is no different from you and me" (146).

In *The Vendor of Sweets,* Chinna Dorai, who takes Jagan to a secluded spot outside the town, says this about his master's way of life:

> People were afraid to come here because of snakes, but my master loved them and never approved of clearing the wild growth around. This tree was full of monkeys. "I'll share the fruits of those trees with them," he used to say. He enjoyed the company a snakes and monkeys and everything. Once there was even of cheetah in the undergrowth. "We must not monopolise this earth...", he used to say. (117)

In Narayan's world, such people who stand about the peripheries of society are more numerous than one notices at first. It is perhaps because they are introduced rather casually and without the burden of the "metaphysical." Consider, for example, an episode in *The Vendor of Sweets.* Young Jagan and his wife are being taken to Santana Krishna (the deity who grants progeny to devotees) on the Badri Hill. The journey is by bus. Jagan sits next to his father, and on the other side of Jagan sits a "threshold" figure: "On Jagan's other side there was a man from the forest with a string of bead round his neck, holding on his lap a small wooden cage containing a mottled bird, which occasionally let out a cry, sounding like doors moving on ancient, uncoiled hinges" (176).

The figure is a combination of a small-statured sanyasis, a petty circus-performer, a tribal, and a soothsayer. The vehicle holds fifty

passengers, double the number it can legally accommodate. Since one
of the passengers is sick, the bus stops every now and then for him to
lean out and relieve himself. It is an impressively slow-progressing
society, containing representations from almost all its sections. And
every time the forest-man's bird gives out a cry, it drowns the conversation
of the passengers : "Remarks, enquires' advice, announcements, the
babble of men's talk, women's shrill voices and children crying or
laughing formed a perfect jumble and medley of sounds *constantly
overwhelmed by the shriek* let out by the mottled bird" (176). The
expression "constantly overwhelmed" is to be noted, for there is a need
to recognise the ability of the peripheral characters to "overwhelm."
One such overwhelming presence is that of the Vagrant in *The Vendor
of Sweets*. He goes down the streets late in the night, crying at every
door, "O good mother, give a handful of rice for this hungry one," and
he has a voice that easily reaches the innermost recesses of any house:
"He had a deep voice which penetrated the door and reached the
kitchen beyond; his tone also quietened troublesome children as he was
described to be a man with three eyes" (22). Jagan has often asked him,
"Your are sturdy; why don't you seek work?" The unfailing reply is,
"When have I the time, master? By the time I have gone round begging
and returned here, the day is over" (89). This man, who is too busy
to do any work, provides the frame, as it were, to Jagan's routine, life:
Jagan meets him in the morning as he goes out to his shop and again
as he returns home late in the evening after closing his shop. He
narrates to this Vagrant numerous pictures of America (the Grand
Canyon is one of them) as described in his son's letters — and even
mentions his son's plans for opening a factory.

Narayan's world — whether its social texture is thin or
otherwise — is convincing, compelling, because most of his people are
not so much characters as figures, or characters aspiring to become
figures. Narayan's preference for "figures" is quite in consistence with
his reverence for the liminal. This is what he says (something that most
Indians would reiterate) in his Introduction to *A Tiger for Malgudi:*)
"when one becomes sanyasi, one obliterates one's past. A sanyasi is to
be taken as he is *at the moment.* You never ask a sanyasi about his
earlier life. He has freed himself from all possessions and human ties"
(9). The sanyasi within the novel attests to this belief : "My past does
not exist for me, nor a future. *I live for the moment* and that awareness
is enough for me. I have erased from my mind my name and identity
and all that it implies" (171).

Narayan's characters aspire to become such liminal figures because of an inner compulsion. Such a passage from a full-fledged social status to a peripheral condition appears to be the inevitable destiny of every person in the fictional world of Narayan. "God knows I need a retreat," says Jagan to Chinna Dorai in *The Vendor of Sweets*, "at some stage in one's life one must uproot oneself from the accustomed surroundings and disappear so that others may continue in peace." To which the bearded man approvingly replies, "It would be the most accredited procedure according to our scriptures—husband and wife must vanish into the forest at some stage in their lives, leaving the affairs of the world to younger people" (126).

Even as a confrontation between him and his disobedient son Mali takes place, Jagan feels that his own identity is undergoing a change, and he reminds himself that "one ought not to resist when circumstances pushed one across the threshold of a new personality" (126). Retirement becomes, for him, a magic word. "If one had to shake off things, one did it unmistakably, completely, without leaving any loophole or a path back" (182). We do not, however, feel that this decision to retreat is escapist or even abrupt, because the play of liminality in Narayan is concerned with *creating* a world and not erasing one, An episode in *The Vendor of Sweets* should amply illustrate this. Jagan's father is a practical man of the world who knows how to get a good coconut crop: "Show me the man who can grow a coconut tree properly, and I will show you one with a practical head on his shoulders," is his constant boastful remark. Yet such a man must make a trip to the liminal environment of Lord Santana Krishna because his daughter-in-law, coming from a family of one hundred and three members, is childless; and a visit to Santana Krishna temple is "The only known remedy for barrenness in women" (171). The temple itself is located on Badri Hill, the base of which is twenty tedious miles away from Malgudi. "Ten months in the year it is raining up there," and the area is full of "leeches and such things" (174). The liminal nature of the god who grants progeny is further comically stressed by a rule that Jagan's father has to respect: pilgrims are not permitted to take coconuts from their own places to the temple but must buy them at the temple gate. Hence Jagan's father, an expert in coconut cultivation, pays an exorbitant price for a single coconut at the temple. He must grudge a little extra expense, says the coconut woman, for he will be rewarded with a grandson, she prophesies. The prophecy is fulfilled, of course, with the

birth of Mali, who increases the number of family members on his
mother's side to a hundred and four. So, then, celebration of life within
society has been made possible — but ironically by a trip to the fringes
of the social order.

In Narayan's world, people seem to be placed on paths that lead
to the peripheries of society. Raju (in *The Guide*), Jagan (in *The Vendor
of Sweets*), the anonymous sanyasi (in *A Tiger for Malgudi*) have all,
before making a final departure from society, made tentative ventures
into the liminal atmosphere of prisons. Paradoxically, such ventures to
the borders seem to uphold all that is precious and ineradicably human
within society. On learning that his son Mali has landed in prison,
Jagan comments: "A dose of prison life is not a bad thing. It may just
be what he needs now" (191-92). It is from the liminal position of a
dead man that Jagan speaks of the validity of the social world to his
distressed cousin: "Everything can go [on] with or without me. The
world doesn't collapse even when a great figure is assassinated or dies
of heart failure. Think that my heart has failed, that's all" (191). It is
because Jagan has become a liminal figure at the end that he can speak
with conviction of the society he is about to give up and the fate of his
unsympathetic, non-cooperative son: "Open the shop at the usual hour
and run it. Mali will take charge of it eventually. Keep Shivaraman and
the rest happy; don't throw them out" (191).

The liminal is to a great extent responsible for the juxtaposition of
the tragic and the comic in Narayan's works. An episode in *A Tiger
for Malgudi* should perhaps bear this out. News has gone round that
a sanyasi is living with a tiger. Among the many who go to take his
darshan is a woman. She bitterly complains to him about her husband,
who has deserted her. She had to go through a forest to seek out the
sanyasi, and the three men who accosted her in the forest have relieved
her of her jewelry. This is mere robbery, less heinous, she tells the
sanyasi, than deserting one's family and home. The reader's suspicion
that the sanyasi is her husband keeps growing. The man, however, is
not at all affected by her accusations, but his equanimity is for a
moment disturbed when she refers to one of her husband's mannerisms,
peculiar only to him: rubbing his finger across the brow. Even when
reading a newspaper, he would "hold it in one hand so as to leave the
other free to trace his forehead," and before going to office, if she asked
for cash, "he would always say, 'If I should *conjure* up the money,' and
while uttering the word *conjure*, he'd send his fingers dancing across

his forehead — whether joking or serious, she always took his fingers
to his forehead" (169).

This sanyasi has the same habit. The man's past, then, is not
totally erased! "Don't deceive me or cheat me," says the woman,
becoming bolder:

> Others may take you for a hermit, but I know you intimately. I
> have borne your vagaries patiently for a life-time. Your inordinate
> demand for food and my perpetual anxiety to see you satisfied and
> my total surrender to you night and day when passion seized you
> displayed the indifference of a savage. (170)

The poignancy in her tone as she starts obstinately addressing him as
"husband" is set against his gentle but detached kindness and the
firmness with which he refers to himself in the third person: "Please
know that he left home not out of wrath, there was no cause for it, but
out of an inner transformation" (171). He neither denies nor affirms
that he is her husband. The comic manner in which she detects the
husband is juxtaposed with the tragic failure of the woman to persuade
the man to consent to this past. In other words, the episode is at once
comic and tragic because the man refuses to become a "character"
(through acquiring a past) and chooses to remain a "figure" (by stressing
only the immediate moment).

Liminal figures like these make us aware of a sadness that pervades
Narayan's works, sadness that has its roots in separation. The sanyasi
philosophises to the tiger, "No relationship, human or other, or association
of any kind could last forever. Separation is the law of life right from
the mother's womb. One has to accept it if one has to live in God's
plan" (174). This law of separation seems to operate consistently throughout
Narayan's novels: people drift away from one another and to the fringes
of civilised life; there is a desperate need for a counter-principle to
retain people within the social frame. Money frequently provides such
a principle, however: it may not be morally and emotionally satisfying,
but Narayan's characters pursue it as long as they want to stake their
identities within the social order. It is important for Chandran (in *The
Bachelor or Arts*) to earn money through the agency of the *Daily
Messenger*, and so is it for Margayya, Jagan, and Raju and others.

Narayan's fictional world is populated by people who exist at the
outskirts of society; such threshold characters, paradoxically, validate

life within society; and it, in turn, appears to cherish borderline values; the tragic coexists with the comic.

The proliferation of "marginal" people largely explains the absence of any great sense of evil and the lack of scope for strong passions in Narayans's works.

Works Cited

Narayan, T.K. *A Tiger for Malgudi*. Mysore: Indian Thought, 1987.
— *The Vendor of Sweets*. Mysore: Indian Thought, 1991.

13

THE NON-FICTION OF R.K. NARAYAN

SUSHEELA N. RAO AND K.S.N. RAO
(University of Wisconsin — Oshkosh)

The limelight of R.K. Narayan's popularity as a fiction writer, both at home and abroad, has blinded most of his readers — and even his critics — to the existence of his non-fiction writing. Narayan is the author of some six works of non-fiction, all of which fit into three categories with two of each kind in a category. These are *Mysore* and *The Emerald Route: Passage Through Guru Karnataka*, both a kind of travel literature, *Next Sunday* and *Reluctant Guru*, both containing discursive essays; and finally *My Dateless Diary* and *My Days: A Memoir*, personal records of his life. They also mark roughly three periods of his literary career as a non-fiction writer, in conception and (for the most part) execution of the ideas that go into these books: Namely, the early, the middle, and the later periods. The first two books deal wholly with the state in which he has lived for most of his life, the former Mysore State, now known as Karnataka; the two books in the second category expand into his observations of topics of a contemporary nature; and the last two are autobiographical works with appeal beyond national boundaries. Likewise, the audiences to which the works of these three categories are of interest extend from Mysoreans, or *Kannadigas*, to all Indians and to all readers of Narayan, including the international. There is a progressively rising literary value in them from the first to the last work, and the purpose of this paper is to examine them critically as literary works.

The first two books, *Mysore*, and *The Emerald Route*, are both a sort of travel account and have little value as literary works and less as travel guides. Both are records of the author's personal impressions and legends of the chosen places. As the author himself has said in *Mysore*, "This is *not* a book of facts about Mysore State. It is just a collection of impressions, descriptions, legends and historical tit-bits [sic]....This is an entirely personal record of my tour and studies" (iii). He recounts fully the history and circumstances of writing *Mysore* and *My Days* (ch. 10). *The Emerald Route* is mostly a verbatim repetition of *Mysore* with some additions and changes necessitated by Mysore State's expanding into Karnataka. In reality, the new book "is but [the old one] writ large." In his narration of the legends of the places he toured, we see the hand of an engaging fiction writer, and his personal comments anticipate the discursive essayist and weekly contributor to the *Hindu*. Occasionally, his account becomes moving, like his description of the battle between Tippu Sultan and the British army (*Mysore* 80-88). There is also in *Mysore,* as Syd Harrex has noted (74), the germ of the play *Watchman of the Lake,* which appears in *The Emerald Route* (115-26); but as a dramatic piece, Watchman lacks appeal and is ineffectual. As travel guides, the books are of little help to would-be travellers, though they certainly excite the imagination to those who know the places described.

"I have," confessed Narayan, "always been drawn to the personal essay in which you could see something of the author himself" *(Writer's* 8). One of Narayan's ardent desires was thus to write discursive essays, and his two books, *Next Sunday* and *Reluctant Guru,* are an ample expression of the fulfilment of this desire. They contain essays selected from those originally written for the Sunday edition of the *Hindu* for about twenty years and for magazines both within India and outside, and selections from these books and others are put together in *A Writer's Nightmare* and *A Story-Teller's World.* Inspired by notable English essayists like Charles Lamb, these essays, avowedly espousing the cause of the common man in most cases, cover widely varying topics of interest to readers of the times and successfully articulate the thoughts and feelings of the English-educated Indians of a southern part of India (reflecting even some of their English). Marked by simplicity of sentence structure, uncomplicated language without daunting depth of thought, chatty but felicitous style, apt diction (including some Indian words and expressions), pleasing brevity, and (above all) enlivening observations spiced with a frequent touch of pungent humour, irony, or wit, these essays make for ideal relaxed Sunday reading. However, they arrest the reader's attention now and again by a sententious thought, an epigrammatic saying, or a Baconian pithiness. Eventually, Narayan says, he grew tired of this "eight-hundred-word expression....This weekly grind" (*My Days* 152).

Several of the essays expound Narayan's sustained and unbroken loyalty to English and its need for India. It is a recurring theme on which he keeps harping. In *A Story-Teller's World* he unabashedly advocates English for all across the length and breadth of the country. With a spurious claim that English is Indian, or *swadeshi,* and yet arguing that English should be Indianised, Narayan is obviously unperturbed by the fact that the structure of a language dictates the structure of one's thinking (and therefore of the mind), a fact that raises the question. Do we want to think like the English? It is a bit bizarre to suggest that a country with its sixteen official languages and more cannot adequately express its Indian mode of thinking and cultural thoughts in its own languages but needs to hanker after a conqueror's language (making a specious difference between the imperialist and his language) and to plead for the Indianisation of English even though such a hybrid is intrinsically incapable of imbinding the Indian ethos, much less express it. Put in a nutshell, Narayan's position is, what is good for me is good for all India.

Narayan's *Next Sunday: Sketches,* a collection of fifty-five essays, reveals his capacity to choose a wide variety of topics and make worthwhile observations using varied approaches to his topics; and a look at some of the essays illuminates the point. In the title essay, strangely placed near the end of the book, he laments the brevity of Sunday and its overcrowded schedule, balking the plans already made for Sunday but fortunately not extinguishing the eternal hope for the interminable return of the next Sunday. " Government Music" is a biting satire on Indian bureaucratic procedures and India's policy of nationalising virtually everything. The sharp practices of astrologers and street fortune-tellers, who exploit credulous people, are deftly exposed in "Prophets in Our Midst." "Allergy" is a playful exercise of pure wit, and "The Need for Silence" is a scathing comment on the incurable itch of political speakers and their haranguing. His "Two-way Democracy" makes an impish suggestion for "de-election" by voters, or recalling unwanted politicians already elected. The essay "On knowledge" is cleverly built around the paradox: " The test of a man's worth will ultimately have to be not how much he knows, but how much he has avoided knowing" (118). The solemn dissertation on the donkey focuses on the sad plight of a docile animal. "A Bookish Topic" is a skilful analysis of the ploy of the artful dodger who is unwilling to return the books he has borrowed; "Tears of Crocodile" is a whimsical essay in which the crocodile, much maligned by man and sought for its skin, artfully tells its side of the story. "Headache" is a capricious essay diagnosing the diplomatic subterfuge used commonly to detach oneself from a disagreeable duty. Finally, "Upstartism" is a study of human behaviour as seen in an upstart, who is described in the following words:

> He has not the slightest doubt that he is the bearer of all the light that the world needs. His views on himself are well defined and may be had for the asking. He feels that humanity needs his wise guidance very moment. He feels that he can have his say in any matter and in any manner he chooses. He is ever prepared to tell everyone what to do and how to do it. If he gets an opportunity, he will not hesitate to tell an expert musician how to sing, an engineer how to build, a gardener how to plant, a general how to fight, a clown how to amuse, and God himself how to manage the universe. (177)

This, of course, is in the great tradition of the British essayists and bears a remarkable likeness to the style and manner of Addison and Steele, Lamb and Goldsmith.

The collection *Reluctant Guru* (forty essays) is further testimony to Narayan's ability to write engagingly on any topic of his choice relevant to Indians. The title essay reveals his reluctance to play the all-knowing at a Midwestern university in America before the students and faculty (who were concerned with learning whether the stories, character, and places, and the mystic experience of his novels are real) and his evasive answers. More importantly, his essay "Children" shows his concern for children in India, who are poorly treated by their elders; but in *A Writer's Nightmare* he comments that Indian children in America, who are well treated, grow up "without....gentleness and courtesy and respect for parents" (239). In both "A Trouble-free World" and Musical Musings" he indulges in an inquisitive mood. His "Indignation" contains some curious statements with a Baconian ring to them, such as "Indignation is the birthright of every human being, and no one can deny another this privilege" (114). "Murder of Pleasure" is a thought-provoking study in which he wonders how a detective story, which begins with a murder, and a tragedy, which concludes with a killing, can be a source of pleasure. In a characteristic manner, he pokes gentle fun at Indian bureaucracy in "A Ministry of Worry." "Our Prossessions" is a humorous comment on people's all-too-common foible of acquiring things only to lose them or their use. In "My Educational Outlook" he severely criticises the Indian educational system and concludes with some hilarious comments made by college students: "R.K. Narayan was a romantic poetess who dies in 1949.... I am sorry, sir, I never knew till today that Lady Macbeth was a woman" (23). On the contrary, "The Greatest Common Factor" is a well-meant encomium of the postman, who, he says, "is the essential human link in any scheme of mechanization.... He is the greatest common factor in humanity. He is the greatest repository of all men's hopes, fears, and joys" (153). Later, he wistfully repeats, "In a civilization of complicated mechanism, the postman alone retains the human touch" (*My Days* 67). On the whole, both books are an abundant testimony to Narayan's imaginative thinking, social commitment, and playful use of wit, irony and humour.

The first of the two books in the autobiographical category, *My Dateless Diary*, is indeed a travel account; it "arose out of a day-to-day journal" kept in the United States in October 1956; and it is not entirely dateless, either; all careful readers can hear the travel clock tick throughout; they can also see the unmistakable stamp of the master narrator. The only group of readers, however, who may have full empathy with the author is the Indians in America.

Aside from its general interest, *My Dateless Diary* is informative on Narayan as a practising writer and the American response to his works. We see him as a diligent and conscious writer — writing, reading, and constantly revising his manuscript while on his sojourn even in such unlikely places and times as at a bus depot, during train travel, and others. We find out that he tries out his manuscript before friends and seeks their opinion. He discovers that although some American university faculty know nothing about his works, he has a large readership, as indicated by the library borrowings of his books. His discussions with Aldous Huxley and the fact of the publisher's vying with each other to publish his books as well as their comments, especially on *The Financial Expert*, are all more than gratifying. He learns that what attracted celebrities like Greta Garbo to his writings was the psychic experience described in *The English Teacher* rather than their literary value. His encounter at Berkeley with an American engaged in writing a novel points up what most Americans look for in a novel. "I think the book is weak in motivation," he said, "we don't learn anything about Mahatma Gandhi, and the narrative lacks punch" (116). Narayan comments, "He felt less discouraged as he realised that I was, after all, a writer of weak motivations, and probably no theoretical knowledge" (116). We see that same lack of "punch" in the imagined satirical television commercial he has written. Likewise, his attempts at writing plays, such as the unsuccessful *The Home of Thunder* and *Watchman of the Lake* (discussed earlier), testify to a lack of dramatic power.

Apart from these, one remembers a few odd details in the book: his problems with the phonetics of *develop* (he puts the accent on the wrong syllable and becomes defensive, unaware that accent in English is phonemic, making a world of difference in meaning as between *Daniel* and *Danielle*, *Adrian* and *Adrienne*, *desert* and *dessert*; some egregious errors ("Lyle has a terrific cold"); odd works like *postmistress* and *inmates*; and his inability to distinguish between a graduate seminar and an undergraduate lecture class (he sees smoking privileges in a seminar as the only difference!). But his English, ordinarily relaxed, rises to poetic heights in his eloquent, deeply felt description of the grandeur of the Grand Canyon; and his vignette of Sewanee is fondly memorable. Also, his portrayal of his countrymen in America is mostly accurate.

Finally, a question arises about the authenticity of the wealth of detail Narayan presents, especially in the *Diary*, and about the validity of his account of the government officials' discussion supposed to have taken place behind the scenes, which he says he put together afterwards (ch. 10), much like the narrator in Sherwood Anderson's "Death in the Woods," who says that he was not present when the supposed things happened in the woods. Notwithstanding Narayan's explanation (122), there is an air of tentativeness about that part of *My Days* and about also the details of the letters Govind writes from America in *My Dateless Diary*. Even with a prodigious memory, one can hardly remember every word spoken by everyone at a dinner party and in other similar situations.

The last of Narayan's non-fiction works is also the best of them, and as Krishna Pachegaonkar says, "Anyone interested in R.K. Narayan's life and work can profit from reading it" (185). *My Days*, in addition to revealing his sensitive and observant personality, has a threefold literary value: it sheds light on his early struggle and preparation to become a writer (including his readings); it provides details of the circumstances surrounding the composition of some of his works. For the most part, it is a straightforward narrative suffused with the charming aura of an engaging writer and sprinkled with wit, irony, and gentle humour — and (except for such omissions and embellishments as are natural to presenting a private life for public record) the work impresses us with its transparent honesty and candour. Perry D. Westbrook says, "This book is written with the same quiet, amused, and kindly irony, combined with the same close observation, that has made Narayan's prose such a delight to read in book after book from his pen" (322). We know that Narayan is an observer of details (as any good writer should be), loves pets, is sensitive, and acts disarmingly charmingly with those from whom he differs. The book is evidently aimed at a wider audience than Mysoreans, as suggested by expressions like "a place called Hassan" and does command both national and international readership. We learn that he is an audience-conscious writer and habitually tries out his manuscript before friends and relatives prior to sending it to his publishers. Curiously enough, though better known for his wit and humour, Narayan says that he "loved tragic endings in novels" (61), a fact that might account in part for the tragic content of some of his stories.

Although his formal education was discouraging, Narayan's personal reading was avid but desultory, with most emphasis on English writers and little attention to the stories of his own ancient heritage. None the less, he seems to have read an incredible number of books and magazines for his age; and while his reading was desultory, his writing habit was marked by discipline, method, and a clear goal. He delighted in roaming about in outside nature and also in observing people in the city and made notes about the types of characters he met. He worked systematically every day on his novel *Swami and Friends* and some stories. He found in the people around him characters for his stories (an observant and comic eye needed to stray no farther), and his own uncle provided the prototype for a character in *The Bachelor of Arts*. His goal was "to be a modern story-writer", and he has no patience with the old classics of his country. "I was a realistic fiction-writer in English," he says, "and Tamil language or literature was not my concern" (102). He still has an unmitigated attachment to English.

My Days is also valuable for its information on the background of some of his works and for shedding light on his critical outlook. For example, we are privileged to know that the metaphysical experience of *The English Teacher* is rooted in the reality of his wife's death, of which there is a very touching description. "*The English Teacher*," he confesses, "is autobiographical in content, very little part of it being fiction" (134-35). Similarly, we come to know about the creation of the character Savitri and the writing of *The Dark Room*. We understand that the Sampath of his novel is a real-life character. Says Narayan:

> At Sampath's I picked up a lot of printing jargon, many characters for my novels, and a general idea of the business of mankind in Mysore: all its citizens converging on the market at Sayyaji Rao Road every day, and being ultimately drawn to Sampath for a variety of reasons.
>
> In a novel of mine Mr. Sampath became a film director. Today I find that the Sampath in real life, too, has become a very busy film personality (160).

Again, he gives details of his conception of the plot and writing of *The Guide,* including Graham Greene's suggestion. No less important than this information is his comment on the filming of *The Guide* (with the consequent fiasco) and his strong disapproval of the film-maker's attempt at introducing extraneous elements for commercial reasons, a disapproval he voiced knowingly, forgoing the prospect of a huge fortune. The book also throws light on Narayan's journalistic experience, including his writing for the *Hindu* newspaper and the *Justice*, as well as on his editorial experience with his *Indian Thought*, together with a penitent's remorse for his uncritical acceptance of an unworthy manuscript. Finally, Narayan discloses where and when he conceived the idea of the celebrated Malgudi, but not how he made up the name:

> I wandered about the streets of Bangalore, dreaming and thinking and planning. On a certain day in September, selected by my grandmother for its auspiciousness, I bought an exercise book and wrote the first line of a novel; as I sat in a room nibbling my pen and wondering what to write, Malgudi with its little railway station swam into my view, all ready-made, with a character called Swaminathan running down the platform peering into the faces of passengers and grimacing at a bearded face. (79-80).

There have been some speculations about the coinage of "Malgudi," but the combination of "Malleswaram" and "Basavanagudi" into a portmanteau word is also a possibility.

On the whole, *My Days* is certainly an important work, and its reading is richly rewarding. Perhaps we can best conclude by recalling an anecdote in our experience. In the mid-forties, one of our friends, a student of English Literature at Central College, Bangalore, was one day caught red-handed reading a novel of Narayan under a tree on the grounds of the college by an Anglophile English lecturer of his (the Anglophile has since become an ardent admirer of Narayan and his works), who roundly rebuked him, saying, "Don't ever let me catch you again reading an English novel by one of these Indian writers!" Since those days, Narayan's recognition at home and abroad by academics has come a long way, especially because of his novels and stories; but his non-fiction writing should not be overlooked, for it accurately reveals many different aspects of the author's life and thought, interests and style.

Works Cited

Harrex, Syd C. "R.K. Narayan: Some Miscellaneous Writings." *Journal of Commonwealth Literature* 13.1 (1978): 64-76.

Narayan, R.K. *The Emerald Route: Passage Through Karnataka.* New Delhi: Vision, 1987.

—, *Mysore*. 2nd ed. Mysore: Indian Thought, 1944.

—, *My Dateless Diary: An American Journey.* New Delhi: Penguin, 1988.

—, *My Days: A Memoir.* New York: Viking, 1974.

—, *Next Sunday: Sketches.* Bombay: Pearl, 1956.

—, *A Writer's Nightmare: Selected Essays, 1958-1988.* New Delhi: Penguin, 1988.

Pachegaonkar, Krishna. "A Note on R.K. Narayan's *My Days*." *Indian Readings in Commonwealth Literature*. Ed. G.S. Amur et al. New Delhi: Sterling, 1985. 181-86.

Westbrook, Perry D. Rev. of *My Days: A Memoir.* by R.K. Narayan. *World Literature Written in English* 15 (1975): 433-34.

14

R.K. NARAYAN'S DIALOGIC NARRATIVE IN
THE GUIDE

SURA P. RATH
(Louisiana State University in Shreveport)

In *The Guide,* the narrator's role in relation to the protagonist presents
a problematic test-case of Narayan's handling of contrapuntal time
and theme. The story weaves two threads of time — a past and the
present — in an intricate pattern of pathos and irony that blend into
both social commentary and spiritual criticism. When Raju's past is
presented, often as a prelude to set the stage for immediate action,
Narayan uses Raju as the first-person narrator who offers a retrospective
view of his earlier life in a reliable voice; in fact, the question between
the author and the narrator appears so ubiquitous, especially in the
context of the Malgudi setting, that Narayan *becomes* the protagonist.
When the narrative focus shifts to the present, Narayan assumes the
role of a keen third-person observer, an astute witness testifying to the
authentic social scene of Malgudi — and, by extension, of India —
galvanising our perception of the setting and the characters but also
conspicuously indicting the spiritual malaise that Raju's life and times
symbolise. This triangular interplay among the author, the narrator(s),
and the protagonist helps set up a shifting narrative pattern in which
the three change their roles as the subject and object of our critical
observation. As Raju, the first-person protagonist, solicits our sympathy,
so Narayan, the camera eye, invites our scrutiny and interpretation.

The novel's dialogic design centres on this alternating scheme of
subjectification and objectification of the protagonist — Raju as the

subject/narrator reviewing his (absent) past, and as an object/character
(present) observed by the author/narrator. Raju's role-reversal, also
suggested by his change from an innocuous child into a convicted
criminal and later into a false prophet, draws our attention to Narayan
himself, for as the characters develop identities independent of their
portrayal by the author, in a brilliant twist of irony and foreshadowing,
Narayan himself, like his protagonist, returns to the Malgudi crowd
and silently turns into an object of further critical observation, ours.

Narayan's readers have consistently identified the forward and
backward movement of narrative in *The Guide* as a characteristic
feature of his fiction, though the technique is often explained as an
element of the novel's plot or theme. Ganeswar Mishra, for instance,
holds that "by narrating the story with movements forward and backward
in time, he [Narayan] portrays the full story of Raju who, before
assuming the role of the holy man, was a tourist guide, lover, dance
proprietor, and convict" (100). Mishra goes on to suggest that Raju as
a holy man reminds him of "Pirandello's theme of illusion and reality."
Similarly, Lakshmi Mani suggests that in *The Guide* Narayan is
"experimenting with a narrative technique that serves his comic purpose
of delineating a protean reality that cannot be adequately perceived by
a single centre of consciousness" (81). However, she concludes eventually
that the "assortment of narrative perspectives" and the "multiple narration"
serve merely to "develop the theme" that "existential reality is fluid"
and that "the truth is a sum total of several fictions" (81-82). William
Walsh, likewise, proposes that the "complex association of sincerity
and self-deception" provides "the organising theme of *The Guide*"
(114). All readers agree that Narayan's aesthetic vision is comic, that
his characters must be examined against the cultural backdrop of India's
religious ethos, and that the novel's strength evolves from its representation
of popular culture.

Such thematic approach to the narrative structure, I suggest,
inadequately explains the complexity of the protagonist's character,
because it fails to account for (a) Raju's incorrigible urge to return to
his past and re-play it before Velan and us; (b) his struggle against the
author to bear his own testimony rather than let the narrator tell the
story; and (c) Narayan's strategy of allowing Raju the autonomy of self-
revelation at the risk of losing his own authorial control over the
protagonist. Mikhail Bakhtin's concept of the "dialogical principle" of
narrative informs my examination of Narayan's intertwining of the

objective and the subjective views of the protagonist as well as of the cultural/historical matrix underlying the narrative. Bakhtin makes a fundamental distinction between our knowledge of the object and the subject by pointing to the nature of knowing in the natural sciences and in the human sciences: the object of the first is to know an object; and that of the second, a subject:

> The exact sciences are a monological form of knowledge: the intellect contemplates a thing and speaks of it. Here, there is only one subject, the subject that knows (contemplates) and speaks (utters). In front of him there is only a voiceless thing. But the subject as such cannot be perceived or studied as if it were a thing, since it cannot remain a subject if it is voiceless; consequently, there is no knowledge of the subject but dialogical. (Todorov 18)

In *Marxism and the Philosophy of Language*, Todorov returns to the same point, claiming once again that since all understanding "already represents the embryo of an answer" it is always dialogical: "Understanding is in search of a counter-discourse to the discourse of the utterer" (123). Hence, as we read a text, we bounce between two foci — knowledge of the thing and knowledge of the person — their boundaries defined by "the relation to the thing" and "the relation to the person," or in Bakhtin's terms, "*Thingification* and *Personification*" (qtd. in Todorov 18).

Raju's transfiguration from an ordinary man with sample passions of love and greed and lust into a con man and convict, and later into an abstract image of sainthood (mahatma), charts this alternate process of "thingification" and "personification" in *The Guide*. By shifting back and forth in time, by punctuating the "thingification" process with Raju's first-person narrative — which is essentially an assertion by the character of his status as a person — Narayan evokes our pathos and pity. But, more important, he draws our attention to the rebellious protagonist who refuses to be pinned down by a cultural cliche. The irony of the situation emerges from Raju's double bind: he either accepts the status of an object, the cultural image of a mahatma, and dies of starvation, or he reclaims his personal identity as an ordinary man and embraces his ignominious past, another death. The dilemma is as much Raju's as Narayan's for, by implication, Narayan himself seems to withstand the simplistic, mechanical reader-response toward him as the traditional *Kultur Meister*.

In the opening scene of *The Guide*, Narayan establishes two polarities, two boundaries of perception. The novel opens with a brilliant gambit: we are presented with two characters, Raju and Velan, the roles for each defined by the perception of the other. The boundary of their social transaction is drawn by measured dialogue and narrative reporting. Velan *stands* "gazing reverentially" on Raju's face; Raju *feels* "amused and embarrassed" with the stare and says to the stranger, "'sit down *if you like.*'" Velan takes his seat "two steps below the granite slab on which Raju was sitting cross-legged as if it were a throne, beside an ancient shrine" (5). The reader learns quickly that Velan, imagining the presence of a semi-divine sadhu, has placed Raju on a pedestal and rendered him into an object, an image made of centuries-old Indian notions about sainthood. The man becomes an abstraction, idealised and inanimate. On the other hand, Raju seeks to initiate a dialogue, to talk about his past and that of Velan. However, he moves cautiously in order not to divulge his criminal past, further strengthening Velan's conviction. Velan thinks he knows all he needs to know about Raju; for Raju, knowing the other just begins.

The relative topography of the two characters is matched by that of the surrounding plateau: "The branches of the trees canopying the river course rustled and trembled with the agitation of birds and monkeys settling down for the night. Upstream beyond the hills the sun was setting" (5). The quiet of the sylvan, natural setting contrasts with the apprehension and encounter imminent in the human scene as Raju asks for Velan's whereabouts, "dreading lest the other should turn around and ask the same question" (5). The initial polarity remains entrenched throughout the novel as the pattern of the villagers' effort to idolise Raju is carefully countered by his attempt to disabuse them without exposing his checkered past. The conflict of the story intensifies through Raju's impossible and contradictory aim of revealing his humanity while keeping his personal past masked, because his only means of asserting individuality is his own past.

The ensuing dialogue derives its meaning from this implied exchange of intentions. As Bakhtin points out, utterances have two aspects: "that which comes from language and is reiterative, and that which comes from the context of enunciation, which is unique" (Todorov 49). Hence, the distinction he makes between the *given* and the *created* in *The Aesthetics of Verbal Utterance*:

The utterance is never the simple reflection or the expression of something that pre-exists it, is given and ready. It always creates something that had not been before, that is absolutely new and is non-reiterative, and that, moreover, always has the relation to values (truth, the good, the beautiful, etc.). (299)

Narayan offers us a clear picture of Raju's slow, but inevitable, entrapment by his language. What he witholds shapes the meaning not only of what he says but also of what others say to him and of how they reconstruct the unsaid. For Bakhtin,

[T]he first criterion, and the most important, of the completion of the utterance, is the *possibility of responding to it,* more exactly and more broadly, of occupying with respect to it the position of responding.... The utterance must, in one way or another, he completed in order that we may react to it. (255).

In Raju's case, of course, the "position of responding" shifts constantly, for his utterances close with ellipses, always incomplete. Not surprisingly, Velan and the villagers are tempted to know him monologically by trying to package him as a cultural hero, a saviour, who might redeem them not only from private ailments but from public malaise such as famine and drought too.

The distance between the "given" and the "created" meanings of their dialogue is nowhere better dramatised than in the scene in which Velan's brother visits the swami with news of fight among rival villages over scanty hay at a time of drought. He expects Raju's blessings to empower him in the fraternal fight, but instead he receives the intriguing message that he must carry back to his village: "'Tell your brother, immediately, wherever he may be that unless they are good I'll never eat.' 'Eat what?' asked the boy, rather puzzled. 'Say that I'll not eat. Don't ask what. I'll not eat till they are good' " (87).

The boy refrains from asking any further question out of fear, but thanks to Narayan's omniscient narrative, we get the benefit of what goes on in the child's mind. His eyes "open wide to"; he "could not connect the fight and this man's food to"; and he "felt he had made a mistake in coming to this man all alone" (88). His report to the village assembly reflects his, as well as their, formulaic response: " 'The Swami, the Swami, doesn't want food any more. Don't take any food to him.' 'Why? Why?' 'Because, because . . . it doesn't rain.'

He added also, suddenly, recollecting the fight, 'No fight, he says' "
(89).

Evidently, in the young man's mind, the swami as a peacemaker
merges into the swami as a rainmaker; in so far as the tradition of India
is concerned, the mingling of the two is natural. In fact, given the
public image a swami has, Raju can bring peace; but he cannot bring
the rain to reinforce this public image. His protest against being reified
as a utility tool is at first too feeble to find its voice; toward the end
of the novel, the reifying force is too strong for him to raise the protest.

The problematic voice shift in the narrative from third to first
person embodies this dilemma: it highlights the schism between the
narrator's portrait of the protagonist and the character's assertion of
selfhood, or between Raju's present and past selves. Less than halfway
through the book, at the end of chapter 6, Raju' s voice rises above that
of the narrator, who seems powerless to suppress the character any
longer. Here we have a re-play of the novel's opening, as Raju asks
Velan to go up with him to the river step, and they sit down, the latter
a step below. Raju tells him:

> "You must listen to me, and so don't go far away, Velan. I must
> speak into your ears. You must pay attention to what I am going
> to say.... I am not a saint, Velan, I'm just an ordinary human being
> like anyone else. Listen to my story. You will know it yourself"
> (98-99).

Why this strange direct appeal from Raju to his audience? Why the
distrust of the mediating narrator? Narayan, the author/narrator, does
not withstand the protagonist's effort, either; instead, as the river trickles
away noiselessly in minute driblets, the dry leaves of the peepal tree
rustle, and somewhere a jackal howls — as though in preparation to
hear Raju's story — he lets Raju's voice fill the night. So did many
years ago another author allow Molly Bloom to pour her heart out into
journal pages that concluded *Ulysses*.

In chapters 7-10, Raju does what Narayan does in the rest of the
novel: he becomes the narrator. The whole section is dramatised
through reported dialogues and narrative summaries — but it is monologic,
because the recollection flows like an interior monologue we are privileged
to hear, thanks to Narayan's silently stepping aside. Raju's self-revelation
runs like a ritualised incantation; in mechanical terms, it is an audio-

visual re-play of an earlier drama. It serves as a story within the story, its spell broken by "the crowing of the cock" (208). To Raju's dismay, Velan remains unimpressed. Narayan takes over his narrator's position again, and the rest of the story reports the carnivalesque spectacle that leads to Raju's ironic, but inescapable, death — more grim than that of Kafka's Hunger Artist. Narayan achieves aesthetic distance and reliability, and thus saves the story from the didacticism that threatens to engulf it, by letting the character plead his own defence. Raju's relentless pursuit of truth and his inexorable progress toward death are thus an integral part of the total plan of Narayan's plot.

Viewed retrospectively from the present, the narrative schism between Raju's present and past represents that between his Self and his Other as well. William Walsh claims that there is "an unbroken connection between Raju, the guide who lived for others, whose character and activity were a rejection of otherness, and Raju (ex-jailbird, ex-lover of Rosie the dancer) the prophet surrounded by devout villagers waiting for a message or a miracle" (121). He sees Raju as "a projection of what people need" and "a vacancy filled by others" (121); "The events leading from the beginning to the conclusion of Raju's career, the links between the guide in the railway station and the swami in the temple, make up a natural, realistic sequence" (122). These events, Walsh says, suggest "the apparently hopeless struggle of Raju's submerged individuality to achieve an independent identity" (122). The dialogic narrative of the novel, I submit, provides the clearest indication of the protagonist's strong individualism; it suggests that, however pliable Raju as a young man might have been to external demands, as a character he is very much aware of his "character zone," that area of his autonomy which he guards fiercely against both the idolatrous villagers and the presumptuous narrator. Bakhtin's observations on Dostoevsky would equally well apply to Narayan.

The full implication of Raju's character and the dialogic design of the novel, therefore, emerges from the cultural context ion which the drama is played out. Bakhtin considers dialogism, or the implied "intertextual dimension" of an utterance, its most important, "or at least the most neglected, feature." The importance lies in the fact that

> [I]ntentionally or not, all discourse is in dialogue with prior discourses on the same subject, as well as with discourses yet to come, whose reactions it foresees and anticipates. A single voice can make

itself heard only by blending into the complete choir of other voices already in place (x).

Thus, to understand *The Guide*, we must listen to other voices, especially those submerged beneath the surface tension of Malgudi's sounds, heard now and reminisced; we must actively participate in the dialogue Narayan has created among not only the characters of the novel but also as Bakhtin says the "discourses retained by collective memory...discourses in relation to which every uttering subject must situate himself or herself" (x). The novel, in this sense, offers us an invitation to position ourselves in relation to the narrator and the protagonist, and Bakhtin's dialogical perspective enables us to choose such a position.

Works Cited

Bakhtin, Mikhail.*The Aesthetics of Verbal Creation*. Moscow: Bocharov, 1979.

Mani, Lakshmi. "The Confidence Game in R.K. Narayan's Fiction." *South Asian Review* (1988): 81-89.

Mishra, Ganeswar. "The Holy Man in R.K. Narayan's Novels," *Journal of Literary Studies*, 2.2 (Dec. 1979): 92-110.

Narayan, R.K. *The Guide*. Mysore: Indian Thought, 1972.

Todorov, Tzvetan. *Mikhail Bakhtin: The Dialogical Principle*. Minneapolis: U of Minnesota P, 1984.

Walsh, William. *R.K. Narayan: A Critical Appreciation*. Chicago: U of Chicago P, 1982.

15

CASTE IN THE FICTION OF
R.K. NARAYAN

D.A. SHANKAR
(University of Mysore)

Of all the Indian writers in English, R.K. Narayan is surely the finest
and most authentic in his representation of the national ethos, the
scenery, the sights and sounds, the ambience of the nation — or at least
of South India, which he has made his special domain under the name
Malgudi. There is hardly ever anything that is unreal in his picture
of peoples and places alike; we are constantly aware that what he
depicts is what we are accustomed to, what we know from experience
or from report.

And yet there is something that is wanting in him, and that something
is, quite frankly, wanting in all our Indian writers in English: it is a
frank recognition of the function of caste in Indian society, a society
of historical and strict caste hierarchy and karmic determinism in
which the *bhikku* (the holy beggar) and the *dasa* (the holy slave) are
held to embody the highest religious virtues of humility and self-
abnegation. We must remember that Lord Siva, the most popular
Hindu god (with the largest number of temples dedicated to his cult)
holds a begging bowl in his hand; and Gautama Buddha, the "enlightened
one," mandated a life of beggary for his disciples. And yet the beggar,
the slave — in fact, all the non-brahminical castes, sub-castes, and outcastes — are seldom even alluded to in the fictions of Indians who
write in English.

One of my colleagues, Dr. Polanki Ramamoorthy, delivered a paper a few years ago to the Indian Association for Commonwealth Literature and Language Studies; it was entitled "Image of India," and here are some pertinent excerpts from it:

> Man in Hinduism is conceived in caste. Caste is *jati* or *Varna*; literally, *birth* or *colour*. To be born is to be identified...by the "birth-profession" or "colour-function," the hereditary occupation. Caste is at once man's identity and vocation, his status and function in a divided labour. One is, therefore, born as a brahmin or cobbler, and if a brahmin, he is *bhu-deva* (literally, god-on-earth) and therefore to be worshipped and served; if a cobbler, he is *asprishya* (literally, the untouchable) and therefore to be shunned.
>
> Caste appears first in the most ancient of the sacred books, the seminal *Rig Veda*. In the celebrated creative myth, Purusha-Sukta (the Hymn of Man), the Purusha (the primal man) divides himself into four parts, and the four castes emerge from them: the brahmins (priests) from the mouth, the kshatriyas (warriors) from the arms, the vaisyas (traders and artisans) from the thighs, and the sudras (servants and slaves) from the feet. And the entire lore of the Dharma-sastras, especially the Code of Manu, are taken up with the prescriptions of codes of conduct and penal measures for the castes — especially with the preservation of the hegemony of the brahmins (2-3).

Narayan, brahmin and middle class, well-educated and well-travelled, lives in a country where perhaps ninety-five per cent of the population is non-brahmin, poor by world standards, poorly educated (if not illiterate entirely) and unfamiliar with the world beyond a severely prescribed perimeter; yet he is regarded by a great number of his readers beyond India as the principal interpreter for them of Indian life and culture. His class, culture, and caste make it virtually impossible for him to understand the private (and even the public) worlds of the sudras, dalits, and other non-brahmins who people his novels and stories. *The Vendor of Sweets, The Guide*, "A Horse and Two Goats," and the other fictions are all wonderful creations, but in none of them is the author truly able to write outside the brahmin sensibility.

One of the stories in *An Astrologer's Day*, perhaps "Fellow Feeling," is the only story by Narayan in which caste is allowed to operate freely, uninhibited at the verbal level. The story concerns Rajam Iyer,[1] who is travelling on the Madras-Bangalore Express and is annoyed by the rudeness displayed by a fellow-passenger; he tries to make him behave himself. At this point the following conversation ensues:

"Just try and be more courteous; it is your duty."

"You are a brahmin, I see. Learn, Sir, that your days are over. Don't think that you can bully us as you have been bullying us all these years."

"What has it to do with your beastly conduct to this gentleman?"

The newcomer assumed a tone of mock humility and said, "Shall I take the dust from your feet, O holy brahmin? O brahmin, brahmin, your days are over. I should like to see you trying a bit of bossing on us."

"Whose master is who?" asked Rajam Iyer philosophically.

The newcomer went on with no obvious relevance: "The cost of mutton has gone up out of all proportion...Yes, and why? Because brahmins have begun to eat meat, and they pay high prices to get is secretly....I have with my own eyes seen brahmins, pukkah brahmins with sacred threads on their bodies, carrying fish under their arms: of course, all wrapped up in a towel (54-55).

The fact that Rajam Iyer, the brahmin, triumphs in the end over the muscularly built non-brahmin may not be irrelevant for a discussion of Narayan's attitude to caste, though even here it is (as it normally is with him) ambivalent. When Rajam Iyer boasts that he has driven the bully away, Narayan tells us that a few of the passengers looked sceptically at him.

In *The Financial Expert* we have Balu throwing away Margayya's account book into the gutter. With the loss of the book, Margayya loses his hold on his debtors; and then a thought crosses his mind: "Suppose he announced a reward to any scavenger who might salvage it? Even if it was salvaged, what was the use? How was it to be touched again and read!" (37). Clearly, Margayya appears to belong to a community that is wholly orthodox, one that is governed in its every attitude and action by the traditional, accepted notions of purity and pollution. Even though Margayya's whole economic well-being depends on his possession of "the small red-bound book" that has been thrown into the "black mass" of the gutter ("wide as a channel"), he is constrained by his assumed caste from trying to retrieve his lost property from the polluted water — though he is clearly tempted to do so: when the crowd of onlookers gradually turned away to follow Balu, Margayya "broke a twig off an avenue tree, and vaguely poked it into the gutter and ran the stick from end to end. He only succeeded in raising a stench" (34). But a schoolteacher, observing him, told him to "Call a scavenger and ask him to look for it.... Don't try to do everything yourself" (34). Again, the conversation suggests an ambivalence: the schoolteacher is suggesting perhaps that only the division of labour is being violated and not that matters of purity and pollution are involved; and Margayya's temptation to do non-brahmin work is tempered by those who have gathered around, "Vegetable sellers, oil-mongers, passers-by, cart-men, students... a lone cyclist."

Somewhat later, when Margayya is about to secure for Balu the daughter of a wealthy man from a respectable family, thoughts about his own caste surface: "There was family secret about his caste which stirred uneasily at the back of his mind" (150). His ancestors were corpse-bearers; his father and his uncle had been known as "corpse brothers"; but in course of time — it took two or three generations — they became agriculturists, landed men, and people forgot about the origin of the family, though an aunt kept repeating, "It's written on their faces—where can it go, even if you allow a hundred years to elapse?" (151). But now Margayya's own financial reputation and status overshadowed everything else.

Now this upward social mobility of a family in the Indian caste hierarchy that Narayan registers is sociologically interesting: you will note that there isn't any connection made in the novel between the passages that I have cited; that is, no ions of purity and pollution play little or no role in the interrelationships between characters. They are just there — in mid-air, as it were.

In *Waiting for the Mahatma* Narayan offers a fairly realistic picture of the location where the outcaste live, indicating at least some familiarity with such places on the superficial level, the level of the transient or tourist. The passage reads:

> This was one of the dozen huts belonging to the city sweepers who lived on the banks of the river. It was probably the worst area in town, and an exaggeration even to call them huts; they were just

hovels, put together with rags, tin-sheets and shreds of coconut matting, all crowded in somehow, with scratchy fowls cackling about and children growing in the street dust (23).

There are, however, certain jarring notes here: *huts,* with no great specificity, is used twice before the much more effective *hovels,* with its very definite connotation of temporariness, dilapidation and inadequacy; "on the banks of the river" also suggests something perhaps even idyllic, and this is not gainsaid until the subsequent sentence; and "belonging to" implies ownership of property, whereas such shacks on untitled land can hardly be said to be owned by or belong to those who attempt to take shelter in them. The real anticlimax is the statement that the children are "growing in the street dust"—a poignant observation but without any hint of tragedy.

Somewhat later, we read, "the municipal services were neither extended nor missed... each had a considerable income by Malgudi standards" (31). This is the voice of the omniscient narrator speaking, and it makes us quite uncomfortable to discover Narayan imposing his class and caste values on the *dalits* (outcastes). Certainly, the municipal services —or their absence — could be noted by any value-neutral observer, but whether they were, in fact, missed is another thing, something that involves a very close identification with the characters' lifestyles, experience, hopes, expectations, wants, needs. Within a couple of miles of the University of Mysore there are dalit villages still without running water, gutters, sewers, and the like; and in one (which some of the conference delegates have visited) the authorities did actually build a water tank and provide a tap: but this was repeatedly broken by caste members who thought that the untouchables did not deserve what today is universally thought to be a minimum civic service. Similar affronts to dalits (and to unscheduled tribes and castes in general) are to be read about in *Dalit Voice: The Voice of the Persecuted Nationalities Denied Human Rights.* "Each had a considerable income by Malgudi standards": what this means, of course, is hard to fathom. If these outcastes had a considerable income, one wonders why they elected to live in such primitive conditions, obviously undernourished (obvious to even the most insensitive eye), and clearly overcrowded. A "considerable income" is surely a very relative one, and Narayan offers no comparisons — certainly not to his own considerable income.

There is also a passage (on page 31) where the municipal chairman tries to befriend a harijan boy, but his inner feeling is not in any way different from that of Margayya already alluded to: friendship with a harijan is just not possible for a brahmin, for it would involve touching, perhaps, and cross-caste intimations of equality or sensitivity. Purity would be endangered.

Rosie, in *The Guide* is said to belong to the caste of temple dancers, *devadasis,* and it is interesting to note that when Raman of *The Painter of Signs* and Raju of *The Guide* fall in love with women who do not belong to their caste, their mothers take an almost identical response: Raman's mother goes away to Kashi, and Raju's mother leaves for her brother's house. Both disapprove of marriage outside of their castes and have little or no consideration for their daughters-in-law, even for Rosie, whose "life was a contribution to the prestige of our nation and our cultural traditions" (200). Raju's uncle raises his objections to Rosie is very clear terms:

> "You are not of our family? Are you of our clan?" He again waited for her answer and answered himself. "No. Are you of our caste? No. Our class? No. Do we know you? No. Do you belong to this house? No. In that case, why are you here? After all, you are a dancing girl. We do not admit them in our families. Understand? ... You cannot stay like this in our house. It is very inconvenient" (149).

Narayan is obviously aware of the role of class and caste in Indian life and the situations that they create in human relationships, but when we attempt to discover in his work some exploration of the relationship that they bear to characters and their actions, we are in for a disappointment. Caste, in fact, has little or no bearing on the psyche of Narayan's characters: there is no structural or organic relationship between characters and caste.

Margayya's rise and fall, the growth that we see in Sriram, Raju's success—if it can be called that—are in no way related to caste membership. The characters work out their lives independently of their only vaguely suggested caste moorings. I say "suggested" because one is never sure of the exact caste position of any of Narayan's characters. We are only vaguely (or in a very general sense) made to feel, to assume, that Sriram, Raman and Raju belong to an upper caste — more or less in the sense in which we are made to feel that Annamalai and Muni do not. Through an aura of certain set, general beliefs and observances, Narayan endows his characters with a caste status and thus attempts to achieve authenticity; thus vagueness and generalness are exploited to subserve authenticity of realisation. To the Indian reader this is obvious; to the foreigner, the omissions are usually unnoticed and hence the shortcoming is overlooked.

I do not suggest that it is not possible to argue that behind the delinking of the fictional characters from their caste, class, and clan there is a deliberate fictional strategy involved; the strategy — if it really is there — appears to be this: Narayan seems to allow caste to enter his fictions only in its broadest, most general aspect, so that it does not tie him down to too much actuality—to too much social realism, if you will. So someone might well ask, "If this helps one to succeed, as Narayan surely seems to, in achieving what appears to be an authentic protrayal of Indian life, why bother? Why complain that there isn't enough 'caste' in Narayan?"

But the heart of the matter is this: in India, what is important is not so much caste as sub-caste. It is not merely that varna terms like *brahmin, kshatriya,* and so on do not have any social content, but that even broad terms like *brahmin, vokkaliga,* and *lingayat* do not have adequate social content. They really belong to the world of nominalism, with no real, objective referents. It is not possible is actual life to come across a brahmin; one can only come across a *Smartha,* a *Madhva,* a *Hoysala Karnataka,* or a *Kamme.* And it is the sub-caste that decisively defines a man's caste status and moulds his social biases, attitudes and his being itself. Sub-castes are numbered in the thousands.

All of this has been well stated by Dr. Babasaheb Ambedkar, the most distinguished untouchable lawyer and writer of India's constitution:

The castes touch, but they do not interpenetrate...castes are not equal in status. Their order is based on inequality. One caste is higher or lower in relation to another. Castes form an hierarchy in which one caste is at the top is the highest, another at the bottom and it is the lowest, and in between there are castes every one of which is at once above some castes and below some castes.

But this will not be enough to understand caste as a dynamic phenomenon. To follow the working of caste in action, it is necessary to note one other feature of caste besides the caste system; namely, class-caste system. The relationship between the ideas of class and caste has been a matter of lively controversy. Some say that caste is analogous to class...others hold that the idea of caste is fundamentally opposed to that of class.... The Hindu is caste-conscious. He is also class-conscious (161-63).

Narayan, by choosing to work with non-existent, broad types of castes, is forced to leave out all the little local details that go with an individual's actual living that is co-extensive with his sub-caste and class status. When these details are omitted, the resulting writing becomes thin; its social content—or, rather, the density, variety, and richness of the individual's societal activities and relationships —is lost, and there remains in the writing only a pathetically emaciated social reality. Accordingly, for all the superficial signs, one cannot defensibly suggest that Narayan is a realistic depictor of the Indian social scene. The amorphous brahmin of the varna system is non-existent, and the pan-Indian brahmin is no brahmin at all in terms of social reality, if we are not told about his sub-caste, we are left with a metaphysical rather than a specific local character.

It is my belief that most of our Indian fictionists writing in English ignore the importance of sub-caste and class and choose to work with *varna* types alone — perhaps because they are understood by Western readers who are quite unfamiliar with the intricacy of sub-caste relationships.

This absence of sub-caste brings upon Indian writing in English—and the work of R.K. Narayan of course—two disabilities: a thinning of social content, leading to a lack of depiction of the complexity of the national ethos, and a too-easy transcendence of the actualities of a truly sub-caste-structured society, leading to a thinness of texture.

The thinness of social content of an Indian novel in English becomes obvious the moment it is placed beside a regional novel like Kuvempu's *Malegalli Madumagalu,* Karanth's *Nambidavara Naka Naraka*, U.R. Ananthamurthy's *Samskara*, or Chaduranga's *Vaishaka*. What gives such rich cultural density of meaning to regional writing is its direct, living touch with the sub-castes. The actions of characters stem from and are directed by the particular code of the sub-caste that governs them. Moments of crisis put not only the characters minds but also their entire value systems to test, and the characters either transcend their sub-caste barriers and become shaping spirits of a new value-based society or they crumble and point to the enormous power that sub-caste structures can bring to bear on their actions. In other words, characters in the regional novels belong to specific socio-cultural groups; but they also become (or try to reach towards) the typical, the truly representative. It is a process of interaction, of growing and becoming, and therefore dramatic in terms of the social content itself.

Not only do most novels written in English by Indians lack dramatic social reality, but they have another drawback: they begin with "transcendence," with readymade types of the *varna* system, and this deprives their authors of an opportunity to work with what is obviously a potentially creative theme.

By sidestepping or transcending the sub-caste forces that govern Hindu life, the Indian novelist writing in English is forced to make the main motive of his fictive characters psychological, metaphysical, or economic. He cannot locate what is, if fact, the central motive in the social being of individuals, this is why the central urges of Narayan's main characters (like Margayya, Vasu, and Raju) are almost wholly psychological; of Raja Rao's, Ramaswamy's and Nair's almost wholly metaphysical; and of Mulk Raj Anand's, almost entirely economic. None of these writers (and their counterparts) makes his characters work out their salvation with full reference to the society of which they are a part, whereas the regional writers locate the central motives of their characters in the realities of sub-caste and sub-class, of psychological, metaphysical, and economic concerns. (These are, of course, closely interrelated, and consequently the writing possesses a richer, a denser texture — one that is inevitably more realistic and more satisfying to the reader.)

Now, many stories can be invented that have great merit and are not based is sub-caste societies and hence lack what I have called the density of social life, so why insist on it as a significant criterion of Indian fiction? These stories and narratives usually take the form of complex, poetic metaphors (fables or allegories); and powerful as they are, they are rooted in the imagination of some anonymous artists rather than in the life of a community as it is understood and represented by an individual artist. The sheer anonymity achieved by such narratives deprives them of their claim to be works of fiction grounded in the socio-cultural life of a specific community: they could be written by Kafka as well as by an Indian novelist; they have no touch of the local, the provincial, the regional and are rooted in some sort of Hegelian universal. Stories that deal only with universals and not with particular "concretions" should not be considered fiction in the sense in which the term is customarily used.

R.K. Narayan says somewhere that one of his principal ambitions has been to write a novel but not to set his name it— to achieve total anonymity. And here lies the problem: all culture-specific details come in the way of achieving total anonymity; details that go with caste, sub-caste, clan, and class militate against it; these ground the novel in specific socio-cultural milieus. And they, in turn, demand social content and localised texture. Most Indian writers of fiction in English want to have their cake and eat it too; this is impossible: you either accept the actual and present it as authentically as you can or you skip it and write poetic fables. Unfortunately, the Indian writers in English attempt fiction rather fables, and what is galling writers in English attempt fiction rather than, and what is galling them is that the writers in the vernaculars succeed in writing novels and stories that are simultaneously fables and genuine works of fiction.

Note

1. *Iyer* is a brahmin suffix that indicates caste. Proper nouns in Narayan become neutral in his later fictions; for example; Raju, Raman and Sriram.

Works Cited

Ambedkar. Babasaheb. *Writing and Speeches.* Vol. 5. Bombay : Government of Maharashtra, 1989.

Narayan, R.K. *An Astrologer's Day.* London: Eyre, 1947.

—, *The Financial Expert.* Mysore: Indian Thought, 1958.

—, *The Guide.* Harmondsworth: Penguin, 1958.

—. *Waiting for the Mahatma.* Mysore: Indian Thought, 1960.

Ramamoorthy, Polanki. "Image of India." Paper delivered to the conference of the Indian Association for Commonwealth Language and Literature Studies. Mysore, 13 Jan. 1981.

16

R.K. NARAYAN: ARTIST OF UNIFORM SENSIBILITIES

RAGHAVENDRA NARAYAN SINGH
(University of Agra)

R.K. Narayan is essentially an excellent artist of the exquisite portrayal of the twin basic human sensibilities: loneliness and separation. He tries to weave the texture of this novels by framing his characters in the natural order of events; men and women in his novels seem to be in a secret pact with the novelist to acknowledge the very basis of their existence. Narayan's fictional world owes its existence to these two sensibilities, which mould his men and women who meet in their lives temporarily before departing permanently on the ever-expanding deserts of time.

The simplicity of Narayan's style and the traditional tone of storytelling have misled a number of his Indian critics, who lament often in their writings his "circumscribed view of life." Every writer has got his own viewpoint, as every individual has got his own peculiar aim in life: but the main point is how you live in a given situation. The most important mark that a writer secures should be awarded to him for the manner in which he expresses his view of life: he should be judged on the basis of his sincerity and commitment to his self-proclaimed law of life. In his memoir *My Days*, Narayan recounts the painful times he underwent due to the sudden death of his wife very early in his life. There is no scope for disbelieving him when he says:

She caught typhoid in early May and collapsed in the first week of June 1939.... I have described this part of my experience of her sickness and death in *The English Teacher* so fully that I do not, and perhaps cannot, go over it again. More than any other book, *The English Teacher* is autobiographical in content, very little part of it being fiction (55).

As is evident from Narayan's self-admission, his views of life are most cogently expressed in *The English Teacher*. Let us have a look at what Krishnan reflects when he is undergoing the painful experiences of loneliness and separation:

"There is one escape from loneliness and separation..." I told myself often. "Wife, child, brothers, parents, friends.....We come together to go apart again. It is one continuous movement. They move away from us as we move away from them. The law of life can't be avoided. The law comes into operation the moment we detach ourselves from our mother's womb. All struggle and misery in life is due to our attempt to arrest this law or to get away from it or in allowing ourselves to be hurt by it. The fact must be recognised. A profound, unmitigated loneliness is the only truth of life. All else is false...." (116).

Narayan's lonely characters meet only to ultimately separate from each other.

The sensibility of loneliness is the prime guiding factor in the lives of his characters. All the activities of his lonely men and women can be studied properly against the background of loneliness. Although the portrayal of the sensibilities of loneliness and separation informs all of his works, I have tried to see the play of these sensibilities in two of his novels, which have been written at an interval of almost twenty years: *The Guide* (1958) and *The Painter of Signs* (1977) reveal that Narayan has maintained the uniformity of these sensibilities in his fiction.

There are numerous references to loneliness in the two novels. Narayan frequently uses the very words *loneliness* and *alone;* we find, in the first very first line of *The Guide,* "Raju welcomed the intrusion—something to relieve the loneliness of the place" (66). In *The Painter of Signs*, we have a poetic description of the loneliness of the house in which Raman, the leading male character lives. The location of the house richly suggests the loneliness of the dweller:

Raman's was the last house in Ellaman Street; a little door on the
back wall opened, beyond a stretch of sand, to the river....This was
a fairly untroubled work spot, the granite steps where bathers
congregated being further down the river; but for some goatherd
who might peep over the wall, no one disturbed his peace (3).

The opening lines in the two novels obviously refer to the lonely and
instructive natures of the protagonists. The two words *loneliness* and
intrusion acquire greater significance when they unravel the mysteries
that surround the men and women of Narayan's novels. At first sight,
these words seem to be quite antithetical, but they are just like the two
sides of a coin, the two facets of a single personality. Loneliness gives
rise to the tendency to intrude on the characters. It is to relieve themselves
of the unbearable pain of loneliness that they try to intrude unlawfully
into the lives of other persons. Raju intrudes into the life of Rosie the
moment he sees her at the railway station in Malgudi. He is delighted
to find a newcomer who may share his loneliness; he starts scheming
to get Rosie alienated from her husband Marco. The frequent references
to Raju's fear of losing Rosie are aptly made by the novelist. He wants
to look as intelligent as Rosie, who is certainly in every respect superior
to him. Raju says, "I smiled affably, my best smile, as if I had been
asked for it by a photographer" (64). Like Raju, Raman in *The Painter
of Signs* is suffering from being hit by the sharp shafts of loneliness.
In order to escape this unendurable situation, he intrudes into the life
of Daisy, the family-planning zealot. Raman remarks about his life and
home in the beginning of the novel, "What an awful lonely home, he
generally reflected, when entering his house, and before lighting up. It
seemed particularly unwelcome at that hour, until he passed to the back
yard where the river flowed softly and birds on the trees over the steps
created a din before settling down for the night" (29). The sharp
awareness of their lonely existence drives the men to peep into the lives
of the women. Raju whispers, "through a chink in the door," to Rosie
in order to peep into the private affairs of the woman so that he may
evolve a technique to get closer and closer to her. The men try to forget
their worries and feelings of boredom by forcibly entering the bedchambers
of the women. But a strange impulse seems to be at work when they
are not allowed to easily peep into the privacy of the female characters;
they cannot wait even for a minute. When Rosie asks Raju to wait for
a minute, Raju reflects: "She withdrew into her room. I wanted to cry
with all my being, 'Let me in,' and bang on the door, but I had the
good sense to restrain myself " (65). In a similar situation, when Raju

is asked by Marco to wait outside the hotel room in which Rosie is residing, he is impatient and imaginative: "Was he still in bed with her? It was a fit occasion, as it seemed to me, to tear the door down and go in" (62). Raman, too, has inherited a dreadful, impulsive nature.

He is impatient to be united with Daisy even when he is not familiar with the physical features of the woman. He is so frantically after Daisy that it is very difficult for him to control himself: "He felt again a surging impulse to cycle up and visit her, but held himself back.... To pursue a female after seeing only the upper half above the desk— she might be one-legged, after all. But this is not sex which is driving me, but a normal curiosity about another person, that's all" (33). The normal curiosity to know about the other person is, no doubt, a justifiable explanation of this tendency in the protagonist, and the source of this curiosity can be safely traced back to the lonely living conditions of the male characters.

In fact, the charge of sex-obsession against Narayan's male characters appears to be based on unsound reasonings, because sex is used by them as the tranquilliser to release them from their agonising, lonely existence. It is not that the women are extraordinarily beautiful in these novels, on the contrary, they are most ordinary girls who could be easily overlooked by any beauty-conscious man. The only possible explanation here is that to these lonely individuals, these women are the only creatures with whom they can share their emotionally disturbed states. Raju contemplates the physical features of Rosie: "She looked dishevelled, her eyes were red with recent tears, and she wore a faded cotton saree: no paint or perfume, but I was prepared to accept her as she was" (64). Then why is Raju so hopelessly after Rosie? Raju himself whispers it to her: "Because life is so blank without your presence"(65). There are some blank spots in the lives of these heroes, who look for the satisfying figures of the heroines. These lonely heroes can be seen walking to the doors of the heroines on no business at all; it seems as if they are walking in a trance. Raman feels awkward when he finds Daisy standing before him: "The door opened, and there she stood like a vision. He felt confused and once again found himself unable to assess her personality, saw her as in a mist. 'Oh, it's you?', she said. 'Come in.' He crossed the threshold hesitantly, wondering how to explain his business — actually no business" (34). These encounters with women reveal that the men have got their own imaginary girls; the girls they love are simply the outer projections of the girls in their minds. And because imaginary girls cannot share their intensity of loneliness, they want to be united with the girls present before them — in flesh and blood.

Incurable romantics as they are, they show a strange tendency to proceed headlong from verbal intimacy to physical gratification. In their minds' eyes they dream of having physical pleasures with the girls after their first encounters. Raju feels jealous of Marco, imagining that Rosie will be in the arms of her husband, and Raman thinks of producing a number of children by marrying Daisy, to foil her plans of family planning. The men lose control over themselves, even at the slightest touch of the females. The unintentional touch with the hands of Rosie makes Raju go wild: "Oh, that made my head reel for a moment. I didn't see anything clearly" (68). The touch of Daisy makes the nights of Raman sleepless: "He lay tossing in bed that night. She had touched him, and that had set his blood-pressure up so high that he had felt giddy, and her perfume had nearly stunned him" (44). Lacking the moral courage to impress the ladies with their straight forward behaviours, they succeed in getting verbal rapprochement; but they are mad to have physical union, sexual intercourse. They can do it even the cost of their complete destruction. Raju reflects, "I was prepared to ruin myself...if need be"(74). He enters the bed-chamber of Rosie, thinking little of the consequences: "At the door of No. 28 I hesitated. She opened the door, passed in, and hesitated, leaving the door half open. She stood looking at me for a moment, as on the first day. 'Shall I go away?' I asked in a whisper.... 'No, no, go away,' she said. But on an impulse I gently pushed her out of the way and stepped in and locked the door on the world" (78). These lonely figures know quite well how to take advantage of the rare opportunities so that they may melt their pains of intense loneliness into the mineral waters of the beauty of fairy-like heroines. Raju takes advantage of the scholarly weaknesses of Marco, who regards the art of dance as mere acrobatics. He gives to Rosie what Marco could never give her — admiration of her dance performances. Raman wants to take advantage of the godsent opportunity of being left in the company of Daisy when the cartman has gone away to another village. Raman thinks in the fashion of Raju: "This was a god-given moment for action. Man must live for the moment and extract its essence. Every minute becomes a yesterday, and it is lost for ever... he saw nothing, forgot his surrounding, his only aim being to seize his prey, whatever the consequences" (93). Though his designs fail miserably, he is able to gain moral courage to begin with the touch of Daisy's hand in his next meeting with her. Daisy meets the fate of Rosie when Raman forcibly acts in the style of Raju: "And then one heard a scuffle and a struggle to reach the switch, feet and hands reaching for the switch, and a click of the switch" (144). Once the would-be lovers have established physical contact with the women, they desperately try to have them within their arms; they want to forget the world by indulging themselves in the sweetest of physical pleasures. For the time being, they suffer from no pangs of loneliness; but soon Narayan's law of life comes into force, and the men are again forced to suffer the agonies of separation.

The only possible explanation of the separation of male and female characters is that the heroines soon learn that the persons they are living with cannot share their loneliness, and they want to forget their loneliness by submerging themselves into their missions in life. Narayan's female characters are even more lonely than his males, because they are talented girls born into the world with particular missions in their lives. They do not want to forget the intense feelings of loneliness by indulging in carnal pleasures; they try to conquer their loneliness by fulfilling their ambitions. Such girls are not born to love anyone else; they love themselves; they love their primary obsessions. The men are mistaken in thinking that they have successfully seduced them; on the contrary, these lonely females seduce the males in order to gratify their unfulfilled desires. Rosie makes Raju dance to the music. Raju reflects, "My troubles would not have started ... but for Rosie" (8-9). Raju succeeds in penetrating the veneer of loneliness of the heroine when Rosie confides to him about Raman: "When we are alone and start talking, we argue and quarrel over everything. We don't agree on most matters, and then he leaves me alone and comes back and we are all right, that's all" (74). Raju wants to make her feel that art is the common interest of both of them, so that she will not desert him: "I didn't want her to interpret it as an aversion on my part to the art... I took care to maintain the emphasis on my passion for the art. It gave us a fresh intimacy. This common interest brought us together" (109). Rosie loves Raju because he is the admirer of her art; in fact, she loves her art, not Raju: "Suddenly she stopped, and flung her whole might on me with 'What a darling. You are giving me a new lease of life'" (109). This is a prime case of a lonely man loving the art of another lonely person not because he is a lover of art but so that he may not relapse into the tormenting experiences of loneliness.

Daisy, the "zealot on the population question" (57), is a missionary spirit. She is lonely by temperament and has been so from her childhood days. She confesses to Raman: "'I sometimes wished I could be alone; there was no time or place to consider what one should do or think. Practically no privacy' " (128). She tries to make Raman understand that she cannot love him because the very expression "I love you" sounds "mechanical and unconvincing" (126). Because they apparently lack common interests, the women remain puzzles to the men. As Ram acclaims, "I don't know what to make of her, she is a puzzle" (133), and Raju fails to understand the behaviour of Rosie when she turns him out unceremoniously from the hotel room. Like Rosie, Daisy too cannot love anyone or anything in this world except her mission. She tells Raman: "'Let us face the fact...married life is not for me. I have thought it over. It frightens me. I am not cut out for the life you imagine. I can't live except alone" (178-79).

One interesting point with regard to the loneliness of the heroines is that they prefer to be loved in darkness: this suggests that they do not love the men they are sleeping with at all. Rosie loves Raju, either when she is lost in the thoughts of her dance performances or when she is sitting in dark surroundings. Darkness and art-obsession make them forget their loneliness. Rosie says to Raju: "'I'm prepared to spend the whole night here.... Here at least we have silence and darkness, welcome things, and something to wait for out of that darkness'" (70) Daisy is afraid of light and allows Raman to make love only when he switches off the light. She surrenders when she is not conscious of her mission: "At some moments, and moods, we say and do things, like talking in a sleep, but when you awake, you realize your folly...." (180). Rosie tries to free herself while making love to Raju when she suddenly remembers her husband. Because these heroines are temperamentally too lonely, they often remain indoors, and the men (both Raju and Raman) knock at their doors to arouse them from their withdrawn selves.

In both novels Narayan maintains the uniformity of the sequence of events. When the heroes are feverishly after the girls, they meet them temporarily, but the women rebuff their love without any consideration. The temporary separation brings in a happy conjugal phase in their lives when the women come on their own to their lovers. They seem to be too weak to get their missions fulfilled without the cooperation of the men, who try to melt the frozen love of the women with the warmth of their physical passions. Rosie returns to Raju on her own after turning him out of her hotel room. She comes to fulfil the sexual drive of Raju, who is not prepared to consider her possible return to his life. Daisy, too, returns to Raman when he is not prepared to welcome her: he takes her physical presence as a hallucination. These last sexual unions of the principals in Narayan's world prepare the ground for their final departures. They are to remain lonely and separated in the scheme of things of the novelist.

In the realm of Narayan's fiction, the male protagonists are gifted with sharp, amorous instincts, which save them from their lonely conditions, whereas the temperaments of the female characters are artistic: they want to forget the pricks of loneliness by submerging themselves into the pursuit of their missions. While sex is primary for the male characters, it is always secondary for the women; sex may be an end in itself in the lives of the men, but the women use sex to attain fulfilment in their chosen fields of life. Sex is not powerful enough to dissolve the loneliness of the heroines, contrary to what happens in the case of the men.

In both *The Guide* and *The Painter of Signs,* Narayan artistically maintains amazing uniformity of the chain of events— men pursue women; they meet temporarily, realising the potentialities of sex; they separate under unwelcome circumstances; the heroines return to the men in total surrender; the women disappear from the lives of the men, who are wonderstruck at the cruelties of their ex-lovers.

Narayan seems to be in the tradition of Kabir, who in one of his poems describes woman as an illusion, *maya.* Kabir says, "Maya Maha Thagini Ham Jani" (woman is a great deceiver). Narayan's females are like apparitions; however hard his male characters try to catch them, they disappear into darkness. Like Kabir, Narayan seems to say that happiness does not lie in outer objects; one has to look into oneself for real happiness.

The theme of loneliness has fascinated many Indian writers; Amrita Pritam is one such writer of great repute. Her novelette *Kachchi Sadak* and her short-stories "Woh Adami" and "Woh Aurat" describe the loneliness of human most artistically. The sensibilities of loneliness and separation are, in fact, the two most powerful motivating factors behind the working of the characters of Narayan, who celebrates life with all its merits and demerits, limitations and excellences.

Words Cited

Narayan, R.K. *The English Teacher*. Mysore: Indian Thought, 1968.

—, *The Guide*. Mysore: Indian Thought, 1985.

—, *My Days: A Memoir*. New Delhi: Orient, 1986.

—, *The Painter of Signs*. Mysore: Indian Thought, 1988.

17

R.K. NARAYAN AND MARGARET LAURENCE: A COMPARISON

K.T. SUNITHA
(University of Mysore)

"It is better for a writer to know a little bit of the world remarkably well than to know a great part of the world little," observes Thomas Hardy in his *Note Books* (95). R.K. Narayan's and Margaret Laurence's fictions are illustrations of Hardy's belief. If the Indian writer successfully creates a fictional world of Malgudi in his novels, the Canadian writer does so equally well in her creation of Manawaka. This kind of writing need not be parochial, even though setting becomes the backbone of their fiction. Narayan and Laurence have both explained the genesis of their fictional worlds in interviews. The former says:

> On a certain day in September, selected by my grandmother for its auspicious day, I bought an exercise book and wrote the first line of a novel as I sat in a room nibbling my pen and wondering what to write. Malgudi with its little railway station swam into view, all ready-made, with a character called Swaminathan running down the platform peering into the faces of the passengers, and grimacing at a bearded face (*My Days* 74-80).

Speaking of Manawaka, Margaret Laurence has this to say:

> The name Manawaka is an invented one, but it was one which had been in my mind since I was about 17 or 18, when I first began to think about writing something set in a prairie town .... In almost

every way, however, Manawaka is not so much any one prairie town as an amalgam of many prairie towns." ("Sources" 80).

Thus Manawaka and Malgudi have a viable existence in the geography of the writer's imaginations. It goes without saying that Manawaka and Malgudi remain for the reader "a living presence" in the same way and to the same degree that the settings of Hardy and Faulkner impinge on one's imagination.

Margaret Laurence wrote five Manawaka novels (*The Stone Angel, A Jest of God, The Fire-Dwellers, A Bird in the House* and *The Diviners*), whereas all fourteen novels by R.K. Narayan and all except a few of his short stories are set in Malgudi. Narayan hardly travelled out of India until his daughter got married in 1956. It was only later, after his burden of responsibility was mitigated, that he thought of going abroad. He says, "It was the correct moment for the Rockefeller Foundation to think of a travel grant. Finally, I broke off the triangular boundary of Madras, Mysore and Coimbatore and left for the United States of America in October 1956" (*My Days* 56).

But in the case of Margaret Laurence, it was different. She travelled a lot before she started writing fiction; in fact, Manawaka is a modest "town of the mind." She felt compelled to distance herself from the country at one stage in her life so that she could reset her intimacies of the place within broader perspectives. As Shirley Chew notes, Laurence stressed the importance of Journeys "as correctives to her previously prejudiced and distorted feelings about the town she had known as a child and an adolescent" (36). The interviews reveal that several regions, things, and people have close resemblances to those in Manawaka: Clear Lake, the Air Force training base, dance halls, the big brick house, the funeral home, the stone angel in the cemetery, the nuisance grounds, shacks in the valley and their occupants, Margaret's parents and grandparents. Places in Manawaka, objects like the stone angel, and characters (the Camerons, Shipleys, Tonnerres, and McLeods) link the novels.

Even in R.K. Narayan's fiction there is a close correspondence between real-life objects, places and persons and those of Malgudi. Narayan transmutes his experiences imaginatively into his fiction. In an All-India Radio interview, Narayan said that "Malgudi is a small temple town situated on the bank of a holy river like Nanjangud. It is also a university town, like Mysore." The important features of the

Malgudi landscape, like the Sarayu River, the printing press, the Market Road, Albert Mission College, the railway station, the nearby hills and forests have very close resemblance to Kukkarahalli Tank at Mysore, the Chamundi Hill, the famous Mysore market, the Mysore railway station, the Maharaja's College, and the Indrabhavan Hotel on the Main Road.

The most prominent characteristic of Narayan's fictional setting is its reluctance to change. Life in Malgudi moves at an incredibly slow pace: undisturbed by the external world, the main pattern of its life remains the same. The people are so deeply attached to the traditions and ancient customs that they inhibit them from inviting any changes in the infrastructure of their society. When Srinivas, the editor of the *Banner* and the script writer of the film *The Burning of Kama*, remarks, "I might be in the twentieth century B.C. for all it matters, or 4000 B.C., he is obviously referring to the never-changing aspect of Malgudi: it is ancient-looking; its streets are dark and dingy, the buildings are unattractive, but it is a growing town. "Like the perennial river of life, the stillness of its surface conceals the dynamics of its depths. Malgudi has changed in spite of itself. It has grown from a small-sized agricultural town to a semi-industrialised city. The Malgudi of *Swami and Friends* is not the same as the Malgudi of *The Vendor of Sweets*. Even in *The Guide* we see Malgudi passing through various phases of development" (Mukherji 11).

The world of Manawaka, like that of Malgudi, records various stages of growth. The protagonists in Laurence's fiction have to wage a battle against the society to assert themselves. In *The Stone Angel* Laurence takes up the story of a ninety-year-old woman's last days, with flashbacks designed to provide the causes of her present loneliness and fear of death. The Manawaka novels point towards the processes of freedom that need to be orchestrated from within. "Setting and personal lives both become political — not in a strict, sectarian sense, but in a way that emphasises human beings' need for human relationships and their inability to escape from them as well. And these relationships — commitments, entanglements, confrontations, affairs — lead readers back to the central characters and their most difficult of all relationships: the ones they have with themselves" (New 161).

Laurence's major characters — Hagar, Rachel, Vanessa, Stacey, Morag — are all women seeking emancipation from the clutches of their society. The title of the novel *The Stone Angel* is very significant, as the fascinating monument has made a deep impact upon her. She calls it "the most beautiful monument." When it arrived by train, "several men in Neepawa had to move that statue. It came from Italy....There were two teams of horses and quite a number of men. They really had quite an effort to get this statue in place up there at the cemetery" (153).

The remarkable object achieves unique literary prominence. At ninety, Hagar sees "this first, largest and certainly the costliest" tombstone marking her mother's grave; it, like the real stone angel, was brought from Italy at terrible expense and carved from pure white marble by stonemasons who were "the cynical descendants of Bernini, gouging out her like by the score, gauging with admirable accuracy the needs of fledgling pharaohs in an uncouth land" (3).

The most impressive building in Laurence's novels *A Jest of God* and *The Fire-Dwellers* is Niall Cameron's funeral chapel, the original of which seems to be the Simpson Funeral Home in Neepawa. Laurence, in an interview, said: "The funeral parlor was right next door to my home....This was a very mysterious house to all of us, because it was the undertaker's. We used to watch the mourners in black coming out to go with the hearse to the church and then to the cemetery" ("Sources" 82).

Laurence draws upon this experience in her two novels mentioned above; in *The Fire-Dwellers* she writes:

> Cameron's Funeral Home in the prairie town, and Stacey, seventeen, coming in late from a dance, stepping behind the Caragana hedge to avoid encountering her mother, who had come downstairs and outside in her dressing gown and was trying to open the mortuary door, which was locked. "Niall — you come upstairs and quit drinking. I know what you're doing in there. I know you," and the low, gentle, terrifying voice in reply — "You do? You really think you do?" (44)

Even in R.K. Narayan's fiction (as in Laurence's), one observes a few common features that recur. There are repeated references to the same objects, but they function at different levels, and the context in which they occur in each novel has different reasonances of meaning. One

of the most important features of Malgudi's landscape is its Sarayu
River, believed to have been born of a scratch made by Ram's arrow
when he was on his to way to Lanka. The holy river is the pride of
the town; distinguished visitors are taken to the roof of the town hall
to have a glimpse of its sparkling waters. The Sarayu River is a mute
witness to many activities that occur in Malgudi. Friendships are made
here, broken contacts are renewed, and commercial transactions are
decided. It is here that Mani, the fighter in *Swami and Friends*, waits
to throw Rajam into the water; it is here that Chandran in *The Bachelor
of Arts* falls desperately in love with the beautiful girl whose looks
drive him crazy: it is here that Sampath, the printer of Malgudi,
discusses with Srinivas his unsuccessful career. And to add to all this,
the Sarayu becomes a symbol of continuity of life in Malgudi. It
becomes an integral part of the life of the people.

The second most significant feature of Malgudi is the Market
Road, which is the pulse of the town. It is a crowded place, noisy and
dirty. Margayya, the protagonist of *The Financial Expert*, belongs to
the Market Road. He is elated to see more people, because it will
improve his prospects of trade. And then we have Lawley Extension,
which is the most fashionable residential area of the town and is only
a few steps away from the Albert Mission College. The elite of the
town, the government officials, professors, doctors and engineers live
in this extension.

The lotus pond is another important feature of Malgudi — like the
ruined temple that we see frequently in Narayan's fiction. The lotus,
as we all know, is a traditional Hindu flower. (In Hindu mythology,
Goddess Lakshmi is depicted as sitting on the lotus flower.) In *The
English Teacher* the lotus pond exists in the midst of thick trees, shrubs
and orchards, which is symbolic of the co-existence of beauty and
ugliness, joys and sorrows in everyone's life in this world; it is a
universal experience. It is near the lotus pond that the protagonist's
communion with the spirit of the dead occurs in a closed chamber in
Rao's house. The temple in Narayan's fiction is often a ruined or
neglected one, although new temples continue to be built — as the
Subramanya temple in *The Dark Room* and the Srinivasa temple in *The
English Teacher*. The old temples depend on the financial support of
the community, as in *The Man-Eater of Malgudi*. Krishnan's friend,
on seeing the temple, exclaims: "The most lovely ruin you ever saw"
— which reflects his appreciation of beauty rather than religious

importance. He is fully aware of the legend that is associated with the temple: "It is said that Sankara, when he passed this way, built it at night, by merely chanting her name over the earth, and it stood up because the villagers thereabouts asked for it. The Goddess is known as Vakmata the mother, who came out of syllable" (131).

The ruined temple is also symbolic of the erosion of Hindu religious culture, which has stood the test of time and the onslaught of alien cultures for centuries.

This is the physical setting — the river, the railway station, the hills and forest, hotels, cinema houses, colleges — in which we encounter Narayan's characters moving with ease.

The people are not overshadowed by the setting. Narayan is not interested in places for their own sake, but his intense preoccupation lies in populated places. Malgudi without its financial expert Margayya, its printer Sampath, its editor Srinivas, its holy man Raju, its author-journalist-sociologist Dr. Pal, and its dandy Sriram would hardly be the Malgudi of Narayan.

As Margaret Laurence wrote for newspapers, so did Narayan: the Neepawa Press in the Canadian writer's fiction is the *Manawaka Banner*; the United College literary magazine *Vox* and the *Province* are fictional. An arresting episode in Narayan's autobiography *My Days* refers to the novelist's brief role as editor and publisher of *Indian Thought*, a journal that was published with the motive "to phrase our culture properly," to make use of the English language as the medium for presenting our cultural heritage. *Indian Thought* failed, as did a similar venture by Srinivas, the hero of *Mr. Sampath*.

The protectiveness of a small place like Malgudi or Manawaka could be an inhibiting factor towards the development of a writer because, as some critics have pointed out, the milieu that seems to be a small town, a cramped set of quarters, might constrict the artist's view of the world as correspondingly narrow, and that the vision might suffer. Narayan and Laurence could also be labeled as regionalists, chroniclers of town life, and nothing more; but both novelists transcend the limitations implied in such a criticism of labels. Their books prove that they cannot be disqualified so easily and hastily as provincial and nothing more.

George Eliot once remarked, "Depend upon it, you would gain unspeakably if you would learn with me to see some of the poetry and the pathos....lying in the experience of the human soul that looks out through dull, grey eyes and that speaks in a voice of quite ordinary tone" (62). It is this poetry and pathos of everyday life that Narayan and Laurence have succeeded in depicting in their novels. Malgudi speaks through myriad voices, smells and sights without losing its identity. Their achievement as artists lies in their making us recognise the familiar landscape: we feel it and see it and know it to be authentic.

Margaret Laurence celebrated her regional roots in the creation of Manawaka. Such a creation not only helped non-Canadians to understand the Canadian landscape better but also helped the Canadians themselves to know and assess their cultural heritage in the proper perspective. Manawaka becomes a symbol of the restoration of the past. Imprinted by personal experience, the characters and situations are not limited by it but transcend the regional truths in which they are located. George Woodcock calls Margaret Laurence "a Canadian equivalent to Tolstoy" — not in terms of "literary gigantism" but rather "in such terms as writer's relevance to his time and place, the versatility of his perception, the breadth of his understanding, the imaginative power with which he personifies and gives symbolic form to the collective life he interprets and in which he takes part" (138). Both writers, Woodcock argues, have a panoramic sense of space and history, an ability to preserve lost times and worlds so that outsiders can imaginatively apprehend them:

> their characters are as impressive as their settings and their best revelations are achieved not... by the explicit statements of historic themes, but rather by the void, concrete yet symbolic presentation of crucial points of instinct in individual lives, such as the moment in Margaret Laurence's *The Stone Angel* when the despised minister, Mr. Troy, sings the first verse of the Doxology to Hagar Shipley during her last days in hospital. (138)

Woodcock concludes that Hagar's recognition of her need to rejoice and her inhibiting pride are intensely personal, yet at the same time one can generalise her situation into a description of the state of mind of a whole generation of English-speaking Canadians.

It is also Narayan's triumph as an artist that he draws us into the world of Malgudi as participants and co-creators. Malgudi is so effectively rooted in our imagination that we wonder "when we are going to meet next in this town," in Graham Greene's words. As he rightly says,

> We can go out into those loved and shabby streets and see with excitement and a certainty of pleasure a stranger approaching past the bank, the cinema, the haircutting salon, a stranger who will greet us we know with some unexpected and revealing phrase that will open a door onto yet another human existence (vi).

In both these writers, the setting of the narratives describes the general locale, historical time, and social circumstance in which the action occurs. In other words, the physical presence of the place and the people associated with it become the dual aspects of the setting. Manawaka and Malgudi penetrate the fictional world so pervasively that any evaluation becomes impossible without alluding to them as the starting point. The complex pattern of the lives of the characters revolves around the milieu as its centre. There exists a strange communion between the characters and the background. The people of Manawaka and Malgudi grow out of it, live in it, and belong to it.

Works Cited

Chew, Shirley. "'Some true image': A Reading of The Stone Angel." *Critical Approaches to the Fiction of Margaret Laurence*. Ed. Colin Nicholson. Vancouver: U of British Columbia P, 1990. 32-38.

Eliot, George. *Scenes of Clerical Life*. Boston: Houghton, 1907.

Greene, Graham. Introduction. *The Financial Expert*. By R.K. Narayan. London: Heinemann, 1952.

Hardy, Thomas. *Note Books*. Ed. Evelyn Hardy. London: Hogarth, 1955.

Laurence, Margaret. *The Fire-Dwellers*. Toronto: McClelland. 1969.

—, "Sources." *Mosaic* 3 (Sep.1970): 78-84.

—, *The Stone Angel*. Toronto: McClelland. 1964.

Mukherji, Nirmala. "Some Aspects of the Literary Development of R.K. Narayan." *Banasthali Patrika* 1 (1956): 10-16.

Narayan, R.K. *The Man-Eater of Malgudi*. Mysore: Indian Thought, 1962.

—, *My Days: A Memoir*. Mysore: Indian Thought, 1974.

New, William. "Margaret Laurence." *Critical Views on Canadian Writers.* Ed. W.H. New. Toronto: Ryerson, 1977. 8-15.

Woodcock, George. "The Human Element: Margaret Laurence's Fiction." *The Human Elements: Critical Essays.* Ed. David Helwig. Toronto: Macmillan, 1978. 130-140.

18

SWAMI AND FRIENDS: CHRONICLE OF AN INDIAN BOYHOOD

CYNTHIA VANDEN DRIESEN
(Edith Cowan University)

Graham Greene, Narayan's earliest Western admirer, wrote enthusiastically of *Swami and Friends* that it

> brought India ... in the sense of the Indian population and the Indian way of life, alive to me ... 'Swami' is the story of a child written with complete objectivity, with a humour strange to our fiction, closer to Tohekhov than to any English writer with the same underlying sense of beauty and sadness. (vii)

Generally, the appeal of this early novel appears to have remained somewhat unappreciated.

Its autobiographical element is one aspect of interest. Despite the fact that it is now some years since criticism and philosophy have been bidden to take note of the death of the author, there is still considerable evidence to suggest the continued accordance of a privileged position to the writer. Foucault explains this as a continuing mode of privileging certain writings over others and expresses the hope for the eventual development of "a form of fiction which would not be limited by the figure of the author to;" in the meantime, he admits, "It would be pure romanticism were I to imagine a culture in which the fictive world operates in an absolutely free state... still, as our society changes, ... the author function will disappear" (731). That time, it seems, is yet to come.

Moreover, in that type of fiction in which an autobiographical element is particularly strong, it is precisely the persistence of the authorial shadow that imparts a special piquancy to such writings as D.H. Lawrence's *Sons and Lovers* or James Joyce's *Portrait of the Artist as a Young Man. Swami and Friends*, in Narayan's own words, grew out of "the urchin days at Ammani's" (qtd. in Mehta 55), the boyhood days spent in his grandmother's home; but according to L.D. Rubin, even without such external evidence, the impression would be conveyed by "the way the story is written, by the kind of details, by the value placed on certain events, very unimportant events often, which nevertheless are obviously being remembered and recaptured" (397). The impression may be fleeting (as, for example, the glimpses of Swami daydreaming in his classroom, contemplating the unattractive physiognomy of his class-master or hopelessly yearning for a hoop), or even a detailed eleboration of incidents, such as the clash with the Scripture-master or the joys and disappointments of cricket. Throughout there is the elusive but unmistakable impression that "out of the confusion of his past experience the writer creates order and acceptance" (Rubin 397).

As a novel of boyhood, this work has little of the strong dramatic interest deriving from a plot replete with adventurous exploit and unusual incident such as characterises a novel like *Huckleberry Finn*. Geared though it is to the relatively unexciting routing of everyday life and the petty drudgeries of school, an unobtrusive but marked pattern slowly emerges. Swami himself is too young and lacking in self-awareness to evaluate his experience, but the narrative voice (perhaps the adult looking back on past experience) subtly marks a progress. An apparently casual sentence records early, "This was Swami's first shock in life..."(31). Subsequent episodes present a series of such shocks, which operate as factors in the boy's emotional development. Swami is not explicitly presented as consciously learning from experience, but he dies progress. For example, early in the novel he almost confides his fear of the coachman's son to his father, but he "suddenly decided that his father had better not know anything about the coachman's son, however serious the situation might be" (92). Instead, he arms himself with a sharp stone. After his second clash with the school authorities, he runs away and has wild visions of being sent to Trichinopoly or Madras to work and earn but finally accepts that, "After all, I shall have to go back to the Board High School..." (73).

The early episode of Swami's clash with the Scripture-master highlights the innate impulsiveness that appears to be at the root of his troubles. Rajam is driven to remark, "What a boy you are, always in some trouble or other wherever you go, always, always...." (147). His troubles, however, plumb a deeper depth than the kind that a William (of the tales by Richmal Crompton) endures. In fact, one critic, H. Moore Williams, describes *Swami and Friends* as "a gentle, more charming South Indian version" of the British author's William books (8). Swami's experiences are intimately bound up with his schoolboy friendships — particularly his hero-worship of the boy Rajam. The novel begins with a series of minor incidents, each working to its own crisis and resolution. Swami's next predicament, the clash between his attraction to Rajam and his loyalty to Mani, is again quickly and happily resolved. The third incident is really the first of the more important crises, educative in their influence. Swami is deeply confused by the inexplicable hostility of his erstwhile cronies: "His cheeks grew hot. He wanted to cry .... Not a word reached Swami's brain, in which there was only dull pain and vacuity" (31). A moment like this indicates a dimension of feeling impossible for Richmal Crompton's William. Yet, with typical boyish resilience, he is soon diverted, watching a piece of tin float down the gutter. Later he even grows "accustomed to his position as the enemy of Somu and company" (33). This action is not followed directly to its conclusion. A variation in the tempo gives a sense of variety and also establishes a sense of the continuing passage of time. In fact, though the narrative time covers only a period of one year, the impression is of a complete tract of experience, an entire phase of life, as it were. Rajam's visit to Swami's home and the attendant preparations (apart from enforcing a sense of their deepening friendship) conveys the sense of the currents of ordinary life going on around the central dramatic events. Episodes such as the arrival of his baby brother, his chats with Granny, or the occasional domestic exchanges between his parents have the effect of rooting the central figure of Swami in a highly authenticated domestic context.

After exams and the excitement of the holidays, a second significant episode, probing a deeper level of experience, is enacted. The coachman's son's duping of Swami involves him in deeper horrors: "He had in his heart a great dread of the boy, and sometimes in the night would float before him a face dark, dirty and cruel, and make him shiver. It was the face of the coachman's son" (75). Even the physical surroundings into which he blunders as a result are unnerving: "urchins with their prodigious bellies, women of dark aspect ... scurvy chickens, mongrels..."(76). Nowhere is the impression of the routine of everyday life flowing smoothly around the active, experiencing mind of the young boy better conveyed than in the subsequent chapter: Swami enjoys his holiday pranks, suffers acutely from his father's attempts to teach him arithmetic, but Father's conciliatory gesture of taking him to the club brings him, all unexpectedly, face to face with the coachman's boy again and an evening of abject terror ensures.

The next significant episode is Swami's involvement in the nationalist agitation. The outcome of events now grows darker. Swami is expelled from the Albert Mission School. The brief narration of changes (Swami in his new school and the dispersal of his "set" in the old) conveys the impression of a lapse of time before the final and most important episode. The animated scenes of the founding of the Cricket Club, the problems of equipment, and the trials of practice build up the sense of the tremendous importance of the match in the eyes of the boys. Interwoven with these are the details of ordinary life, such as the incident of Granny and her lemon. Swami's attempts at compromise between the intransigent demands of the Board school discipline and his own intense desire to fulfil the expectations of his friends reaches a crisis in his clash with the Board school headmaster. His running away provokes the major crisis of the lost match and the estrangement from Rajam, which is, for Swami, the ultimate tragedy. His misfortunes have mostly been the very direct result of the operation of Swami's own qualities of character and temperament on circumstance. It is only at the very last — in Rajam's going away — that there is the suggestion of the action of an inevitable fate. Moreover, it is Swami's own procrastination in seeking a reconciliation with Rajam that prevents him from learning of it earlier and thus materially lessening the shock. Swami is here confronted with an impersonal situation that makes his own regrets or Rajam's forgiveness seem finally irrelevant. It is a fitting culmination to the widening cycle of experience to which he has been subjected. The physical travail of his experience on the Memphi Forest Road now appears to be complemented by an emotional breakdown. Acceptance appears impossible. At the station he "raves" at Mani, and his cry, "Oh Rajam, Rajam ... when will you come back?" (178) shows his increasing loss of self-control. Finally, he breaks down and sobs. It is the kind of behaviour impossible to Crompton's William, but then William is purely a figure of comedy; Swami seems more nearly a figure drawn from life.

Each of the shocks that Swami experiences has the effect of being underlined through the fact that in each instance physical suffering in some form accompanies the mental experience. In the clash with Somu and Co., there is a hand-to-hand fight; in the episode of the coachman, Swami is stoned; in the nationalist struggle, he is assaulted by the policeman. An ascending scale of severity appears to be depicted until in the last episode he is found unconscious by the cartman and it is only "after hours of effort with food and medicine that the boy was revived" (164). Yet there is no effect of unrelieved pessimism. Some crises (even the episode of his running away) work out to fortunate conclusions: Swami enjoys the companionship of his friends, Granny's indulgence and also his parents' affection, though he himself is less aware of this fact.

The effects of comedy also help preserve a sense of detachment, so that Swami's trials are rendered in perspective. Often it is through the presentation of the exaggerated working of Swami's over-active imagination that the comic effect is created, such as in his imaginative involvement with Rama and Krishna, which prevents his working out a problem in arithmetic. At the same time, this exaggeration functions as a comment, a pointer to his boyish inexperience, impulsiveness, and irresponsibility. Even at the height of crisis, a comic note is struck: "Swami shuddered as he realised what a deep-dyed villain Dr, Kesavan was ... he would not allow that villain to feel his pulse even if he (Swami) should be dying of fever!" (144). Exaggeration, in fact, appears to be the favoured device for comic effects, as in the description of Ebenezer's Scripture class: "Tears rolled down Ebenezer's cheeks when he pictured Jesus .... Next moment his face became purple with rage" (5); or in the characterisation of Mani: "He came to the class, monopolised the last bench, and slept bravely. No teacher ever tried to prod him. It was said that a new teacher who tried it very nearly lost his life" (8). There are also the comic effects that spring from incongruities of situation, such as Swami's reflections on his class master's unattractive appearance while the latter corrects his homework, or the Board schoolmaster found asleep. Inextricably twined with the comedy are the touches of pathos, as in Swami's desperate attempts to scrape together a few annas for a hoop: he even tries magic. Often the pathos derives from the complete indifference of the adults (except, perhaps, Granny, herself a marginalised figure) to his keenest wants.

The final scenes of Swami's parting from Rajam are remarkably serious in tone, underlining the effect of a particularly painful and climatic experience. One has the impression that Swami's feelings are kept under control simply because he is obliged to keep at a distance from his friend physically because of the crush at the station. When he does face him briefly, "Swaminathan lost control of himself" (178), but before emotion can really gain the upper hand, Rajam is whisked away. The scene is quite remarkable for its technique: the mechanics of the action ensure that feeling is kept within bounds, although the poignancy of Swami's situation derives from his state of complete emotional breakdown. The narrative voice maintains a fine balance between humorous detachment and empathy with the central figure. It is apart form and yet involved in the experience of the central character, who is only dimly aware of the full implication of events. The reader is aware of a gap between the level of awareness of the naive protagonist, the boy Swami, and the more inclusive consciousness of the narrative voice. In the autobiographical work this voice acquires the inflections of the authorial personality looking back on past experience. The movement between these levels of consciousness is skilfully effected. In the depiction of Swami's involvement with the nationalists, for instance, in such a statement as "He paused and said on the inspiration of the moment 'We are slaves of slaves'..." (93), it is the narrative voice speaking; but next the focus is on Swami's own reactions: "The persons who cut off Dacca muslin..." (105). The reader registers on another occasion how his peculiar reaction is caused by his vivid consciousness of guilt in Rajam's presence: "The back of his head and pink ears were visible to Swami .... Swami was in intolerable suspense that the head should turn and fix its eyes on his .... If only somebody would put a blackboard between his eyes and those pink ears" (105).

Swami's consciousness of the inimical quality of the adult world, his aversion to the rigours and discipline of school or study, his hero-worship, his impulsive enthusiasms and yearnings (whether for the possession of a hoop or the joys of cricket and the companionship of kindred spirits) refract the universal experiences of boyhood. His dilemmas recall the predicaments of Pip, of David Copperfield, of Huckleberry Finn — fictive characters whose joys and frustrations still affect readers across time and space. Yet Swami (like them) remains, finally, a creature of a particular time and place. He belongs, recognisably, to his Indian environment. When hungry his longings are for ghee and curds; when he is lost; his terrors are of elephants, yellow and black tigers, cobras, scorpions, demons. In his fear, "he prayed to all the gods that he knew .... He promised them offerings ... to roll bare-bodied in the dust, and take alms to the Lord Thirupathi" (160). On a subtler level, the rough, pioneering, independent spirit of Huckleberry Finn is as foreign to him as the sophisticated concern with social graces that occupies the young boy of Tolstoy's *Childhood, Boyhood and Youth*. Swami emerges as a very ordinary and undistinguished boy, and perhaps this ordinariness enhances his representative quality. He is attracted to "the Pea" because of the similarity of disposition: "he was just ordinary, no outstanding virtue of muscle or intellect. He was as bad in arithmetic as Swami was, he was apprehensive, weak and nervous ... the bond between them was laughter" (9). Part of the sense of a "rounded" portraiture (in the Forsterian sense) derives from the enfolding circle of domestic relationships and routine within which Swami is placed, picture upsetting his mother by grabbing the baby's cloth, alternately bullying or humouring his granny, adroitly avoiding his father's eye, or ignoring his mother's admonitions. His peculiar mixture of timidity and boldness renders his actions continually capable of surprising — and yet, in retrospect, completely credible.

The minor figures emerge with similar clarity, mostly in terms of their impact on Swami. It is his visual impression and attitude that colours the presentation of "Fire-eyed Vedanayagam" or the Board school headmaster: "The wizened, spectacled man was a repulsive creature with his screeching voice" (172). Swami's particular friends, Mani and Rajam, are developed in greater detail than the others in this band. Mani is largely a figure of comedy (the element of exaggeration in this portraiture has been noted earlier), with his great brawn and little brain, but with depths of loyalty and devotion in his ravings and is a veritable tower of strength to him, acting as his spokesman and agent, and even offering him consolation of a sort. Even as the insignificant David is attracted to the glamorous Steerforth in *David Copperfield*, Swami is dazzled by the mental and physical accomplishments of Rajam. Rajam's material possessions — his car, his clothes, his toys, and even his father's position — further establish him as a superior being in Swami's eyes. Unlike Steerforth, Rajam appears wholly deserving of respect. His physical and mental superiority is repeatedly dramatised in such episodes as his deliberate challenge and later equally deliberate placation of Mani, his pacification of the faction of Somu and Co., and his calm confrontation of the Board school headmaster. His style of speech dramatises this poise. When Swami makes his excited complaint against the coachman, "He has duped me of two annas ...", Rajam interposes, "My dear boy, twelve pice make one anna and you have paid thrice six pice each time; that is eighteen pice in all," and on Swami's protests insists, "But in money matters you must be precise" (74). The contrast of the character is effectively enforced.

Even in this earliest novel, that the English language functions credibly as a medium of expression for *Indian* characters is amply demonstrated. In the conversation of the schoolboys, their quick animosities and changing enthusiasms, their joys and their disappointments are conveyed with a sense of authenticity and immediacy: "Are you a man ... Which dog doubts it? Have you the courage to prove that you are a man?" "How?" ... "Meet me at the river" ... "What for?" "To see if you can break my head" ... "Oh, to pieces!" (17).

The novel has little overt concern with political and social issues. The illusion of the boy's world is consistently preserved; the political riots do not appear more significant to him than his clash with the coachman's urchin or his loss of Rajam. Yet the reader is also aware of the concrete impact of these larger issues on individual lives. External details such as street names (Lawley Extension, Grove Street) or peripheral events presented (such as the nationalist unrest) are reminders that the setting is an *India* under British rule. There are more subtle details. Part of the admiration accorded is for his European clothes; "socks and shoes, fur cap and tie and a wonderful coat and knickers" besides his ability to speak English "exactly like an European" (45). Swami and his friends are fanatical cricketers. Swami's father plays tennis at the club. Nevertheless, the emerging nationalist pride in *khaddar* (homespun) clothing is symptomatic of new forces at work. Swami's schoolboy world can be directly affected by larger political and social issues; his participation in the nationalist demonstration makes him feel guilty towards Rajam, whose father is a deputy superintendent of police, owing loyalty to the British Government. Earlier, the Pea makes only a gesture of disapproval of the Scripture-master's conduct; being a Christian, he basically approves the master's criticism of Hinduism. Swami's reaction is much more nationalistic in its resentment.

There is, in the Malgudi of this early novel, a definite quality of the idyllic, reflected, for example, in the descriptions of the River Saryu, which bounds it on one side, "glistening like a silver belt across the north" (13). Its other boundary is "the thick belt of Memphi Forests" (157). The suggestion of isolation further enhances this idyllic quality, emphasised also by the constant evocation of the intimate connection with the rural village. Thus, country carts lumber along the Trunk Road and herds of cattle ford the stream at Nalappa's Grove. Swami's route along the Trunk Road is "shaded by trees bearing fruits, the white ball-like wood-apple, green figs and deep purple eugenia pepped out of thick green foliage" (158).

The autobiographical novel, unlike the autobiography, is not to be tested by its fidelity to biographical fact. Paradoxically, its peculiar advantage over the biography is that often by its very departure from literal fact it is able to show the whole truth of a character or situation, the deeper logic or pattern of meaning that ordinary life itself might obscure. Thus Kenny James, though he often took a character or incident from life as a starting point for a novel, deliberately refused to follow the rest of the facts, in which he saw only "clumsy life at her stupid work." In his discussion of James Joyce's *Portrait of the Artist as a Young Man* and D.H. Lawrence's *Sons and Lovers*, Pascal shows how the departures from biographical fact are dictated by the over-rider authorial intention of giving a special pattern to events, impressing motif, which works finally towards evoking a more general and representative significance from events described (133).

Narayan's own departures from ascertainable biographical fact works in the same direction. For example, although much of the material derives from the period of his life which he spent with his grandmother in her own home, a much indulged grandson, he presents her here as a singularly powerless and pathetic figure. Thus the young boy's essential defencelessness against the generally indifferent and inimical adult world is emphasised. Again, where the boy Narayan was one of a *large* family comprising five brothers and two sisters, Swami of the story has one brother — and that a baby. The logic behind the change is self-evident: the focus is completely on Swami; his conflicts and predicaments are highlighted in a manner impossible to achieve were he made to share the stage with a host of sibling figures.

Note

1   This provides an interesting adaptation of two of the three fundamental narrative situations identified by Franz Stanzel as "authorial" and "figural." In the former, the narrative proceeds from a point of view

external to the action; in the latter, the point of view remains with one of the actors. The third category is the first-person narrative situation. See Franz Stanzel, *Narrative Situations in the Novel* (Bloomington: Indiana UP, 1971). These relatively simple schema admit of a remarkable degree of elaboration, as shown by Gerard Genette, *Narrative Discourse* (Oxford: Blackwell, 1980).

Works Cited

Foucault, Michel. "What is an Author?" *Literary Criticism and Theory.* Ed. Robert Con Davis and Laurie Finke. New York: Longmans, 1991. 729-35.

Greene, Graham. Introduction. *The Bachelor of Arts.* By R.K. Narayan. London: News,   1951. v-viii.

Mehta, Ved. "Profiles: The Train Had Just Arrived at Malgudi Station." *New Yorker* 38 (15 Sep 1962): 53+.

Narayan, R.K. *Swami and Friends.* Mysore: Indian Thought, 1971.

Pascal, L. "The Autobiographical Novel and the Autobiography." *Essays in Criticism.*9 (1959): 141-45.

Rubin, L.D. "The Self Re-captured." *Kenyon Review* 25.3 (Summer 1963): 391-99.

Williams, H. Moore. ""English Writing in Free India, 1946-1967." *Twentieth-Century Literature* 16.1 (Jan. 1970): 1-12.